365 No or Low Cost Workplace Team Building Activities

Games and Exercises Designed to Build Trust and Encourage Teamwork Among Employees

First Edition by John Peragine
Revised by Grace Hudgins

365 NO OR LOW COST WORKPLACE TEAM BUILDING ACTIVITIES: GAMES AND EXERCISES DESIGNED TO BUILD TRUST AND ENCOURAGE TEAMWORK AMONG EMPLOYEES

Copyright © 2017 Atlantic Publishing Group, Inc.

1405 SW 6th Avenue • Ocala, Florida 34471 • Phone 800-814-1132 • Fax 352-622-1875

Website: www.atlantic-pub.com • Email: sales@atlantic-pub.com

SAN Number: 268-1250

Library of Congress Cataloging-in-Publication Data

Names: Peragine, John N., author. | Hudgins, Grace, author.
Title: 365 low or no cost workplace teambuilding activities : games and
  exercises designed to build trust and encourage teamwork among employees /
  by John Peragine ; revised by Grace Hudgins Other titles: Three hundred sixty five low or no cost workplace teambuilding
  activities
Description: Revised 2nd edition. | Ocala, Florida : Atlantic Publishing
  Group, Inc., [2016] | Includes bibliographical references and index.
Identifiers: LCCN 2015036709| ISBN 9781620230671 (alk. paper) | ISBN
  1620230674 (alk. paper)
Subjects: LCSH: Teams in the workplace. | Interpersonal communication. |
  Communication in organizations.
Classification: LCC HD66 .P427 2016 | DDC 658.4/022--dc23 LC record available at https://lccn.loc.gov/2015036709

Printed in the United States

PROJECT MANAGER AND EDITOR: Rebekah Sack • rsack@atlantic-pub.com
INTERIOR LAYOUT AND JACKET DESIGN: Diana Russell • dianarussell@diana-russell-design.com
COVER DESIGN: Jackie Miller • millerjackiej@gmail.com

Reduce. Reuse.
RECYCLE.

A decade ago, Atlantic Publishing signed the Green Press Initiative. These guidelines promote environmentally friendly practices, such as using recycled stock and vegetable-based inks, avoiding waste, choosing energy-efficient resources, and promoting a no-pulping policy. We now use 100-percent recycled stock on all our books. The results: in one year, switching to post-consumer recycled stock saved 24 mature trees, 5,000 gallons of water, the equivalent of the total energy used for one home in a year, and the equivalent of the greenhouse gases from one car driven for a year.

Over the years, we have adopted a number of dogs from rescues and shelters. First there was Bear and after he passed, Ginger and Scout. Now, we have Kira, another rescue. They have brought immense joy and love not just into our lives, but into the lives of all who met them.

We want you to know a portion of the profits of this book will be donated in Bear, Ginger and Scout's memory to local animal shelters, parks, conservation organizations, and other individuals and nonprofit organizations in need of assistance.

– Douglas & Sherri Brown,
President & Vice-President of Atlantic Publishing

Table of Contents

CHAPTER 6 - COMMUNICATION IS THE KEY: LISTENING AND TALKING EXERCISES FOR YOUR TEAM   151

In-House Trainings   151

Company Retreats   160

Foreword

Team building demands patience, persistence, and continuous evolution. Games and exercises function to stress the importance of certain aspects of effective teams: trust, communication, and cultural awareness, just to name a few. Taking those lessons into daily work demands that leaders exemplify the qualities they seek to instill across the team.

My earliest lessons in team building and leadership began in the humblest of jobs — as a teenager washing dishes in a locally-owned Italian restaurant and pizzeria in Upstate New York. The owner insisted that he would never give a task to an employee that he would not also do himself. By jumping into a dumpster with brushes, soap, and a hose; or diving into the huge pile of dishes during a Friday night rush; or tossing flattened dough high into the air, he lived his words. His philosophy and actions instilled respect for him from all the employees. When he asked a staff member for assistance in a task, we saw that he operated transparently and humbly. We always complied without complaint.

The drawback of that lesson is that it's culture-bound and rooted in American independence with appeal to equality and accountability among team members. When my career path placed me managing a team of 16 employees across the world in Kenya, that down-to-earth style conflicted with strong hierarchical tendencies and respectful submission to authority. I recognized that my responsibility as a leader demanded that I change to lead that team, although I could not fully shift my basic philosophy. Over my first year with the Kenyan team, I learned which employees embraced more authority and decision making and those that functioned best with a direct, command-style approach.

A leader must recognize that each team is unique, and in our multi-cultural society, each team member will bring along cultural assumptions. Some of the exercises in this edition are designed to highlight those differences to aid teams in being more effective as they adjust to each other.

Remote teams pose specific challenges for leaders, and with pervasive technology that allows team members to work from wherever they are, leaders must foster trust. This is essential. But how? Be responsive, be accessible, be flexible, be inclusive — particularly with communications — and keep a good sense of humor. With a remote team spanning the U.S. from Seattle to Tampa, I erred multiple times presuming I understood a written comment or question when, in fact, the author had very different intentions. I found myself fuming, only to realize later that my interpretation veered wildly from the team member's meaning. Now when that occurs, I've learned to call or to speak via online face-to-face technology — not respond in writing — and seek clarification. This volume provides leaders informative and practical activities to help bring remote teams together in a virtual sense.

In using this book, take stock of which exercises are suitable for your team, their personalities, and the needs of your organization at the time you develop or adapt the activity. Understand that the game or exercise ignites the beginning of the change you seek and that your daily interactions with team members must also reinforce the quality or value behind the game's purpose. Most of all, be open to truly hearing your team's responses and reactions in the debrief as you will glean valuable insights to propel you to be a better leader tomorrow than you are today.

—Dr. Shawn J. Woodin

Dr. Woodin's career spans higher education, non-profits, international education, and community development. He earned his Doctorate in Higher Education Administration at the University of Florida while directing a scholarship program for international students to study at U.S. community colleges. His professional work has brought him to countries in Europe, South America, and Africa thus far, including nearly six years living in Kenya. He is currently President/CEO of the Southern Scholarship Foundation in Tallahassee, Florida.

Introduction

"The success of teamwork: Coming together is a beginning; keeping together is progress; working together is success."
—Henry Ford

As Henry Ford quoted above, teamwork is not about going through the motions. It's not even about the end result. It's about the bond your team members create while putting in hard work toward their end goal.

Before you pick out the best team building exercises for your team, think about why you want to do them in the first place. Do you have a new team? Are there certain areas within your team that need improvement? Once you've narrowed that down it will be much easier to use this book as a guide.

The rest of the book's activities have been categorized into chapters based off improvement areas such as communication, trust, collaboration, and team bonding. It's now easier to find an activity that you think will work best for your team.

The second edition of this book includes more team building activities for teams that telecommute or work from home. Technology has influenced today's workforce — so much so that a large percent now works remotely and is self-employed by doing so. Chapter 11 is dedicated to such virtual teams — big or small — and how technology can bring those teams just as close as in-person teams.

It also includes more activities that highlight the importance of diversity, breaking down stereotypes and acceptance. According to a 2015 report conducted by CareerBuilder, the number of women, Hispanics, and Asians increased in the U.S. workforce, and African Americans gained 44 percent of the job market in higher paying careers like surgeons, airline pilots, and purchasing managers. By 2050, the U.S. Center for American Progress reports that there will be no racial or ethnic majority in the country. To promote more diversity, acceptance, and recognition for these diversity factors, multiple team building activities that break down stereotypes against religions, ethnicities, and genders have been added.

TEAM LEADERS

The work ethic, skill, and attitude that each individual member brings to a team is what make it successful. However, members and employees are not what make the team function entirely — team leaders are just as important. Without the direction, organization, and intelligence team leaders should possess, the team would not reach its goals or complete its tasks.

It's important for the team leader to be the prime example for his or her team. That way, employees can observe the leadership style he or she uses to complete everyday tasks. By observing, they will learn new skill sets from their boss, learn his or her expectations, and potentially learn the ideal qualities to become a leader one day.

Before we get into team building activities, it's important for you to understand the makings of a great leader. These qualities are great to revisit, if even you think you don't need to, before getting your team to bond and participate in exercises that involve communication and trust.

ROLE MODEL

As we mentioned above, a leader must be a dynamic and powerful role model, a person the team wants to emulate. Ideally, this person will not only be well qualified but also have significant experience. A leader should have a strong reputation, strong ethics, and inspire those a part of the team. It is difficult for a leader to ask his or her members to accomplish things that he or she is not able or willing to do. So as the leader, CEO, manager, boss, or whatever title suits you, it's important for you to portray the skills and attitude you would want your employees to portray as well.

PERSONALITY

Ambitious planning and execution are essential qualities, but they will not get a team very far if members are unwilling to cooperate with the leader. Many people with excellent leadership skills fail because they are unable to achieve buy-in. If individuals are committed to the goals laid down by their leader, the goals are much easier to achieve. If they are not, very little will be accomplished. The leader must be likeable, personable, a good listener, compassionate in dealings with his people, and flexible enough that everyone is comfortable with his or her leadership. If the team members genuinely like and admire him or her, they will follow him or her anywhere. In dealing with territorial issues, jealousy, or competitiveness, a winsome personality goes a long way toward solving serious conflicts. If a leader is hired from within and has a negative relationship with his or her peers, or a history of not following directions, the chance of that behavior changing is not likely if he or she is promoted.

COMMITMENT

An effective leader is one who believes he or she can make a difference and is so committed to the cause that it's obvious to stakeholders. The leaders must believe in the value of what the team does and be unfailingly committed to its mission and goals. Otherwise, he or she will not be able to inspire the members of the team to catch the fire of commitment. Leaders should believe that the group can make a difference. Their passion should be especially evident in the type of language and attitude they show on a daily basis.

COOPERATION

Some people are, by their nature, obstinate when it comes to getting along with others. This is not a characteristic that leads to effective leadership. A good question to ask in becoming a leader is whether you exhibit a cooperative spirit. Are you willing to listen to others' opinions and ideas and, at times, replace them with your own along with new or better approaches? Everyone has a voice, and people make stronger team members if they are able to contribute more than just their time and effort. A good leader will recognize this and value it in their team members.

OPTIMISM

The effective leader keeps his team members' spirits up even in the event of disappointment. The leader must believe that established goals are going to be achieved and that any roadblock can be overcome. If the leader does not believe this, then the team will not either. A leader sets the tone and atmosphere for his or her team. If he or she is negative, then the team will follow suit. If, on the other hand, he or she is positive, smiles, talks about how much the team is accomplishing, and identifies individuals' successes, then the team will be positive and motivated to work harder.

SELF-KNOWLEDGE

Nothing puts a damper on a team more than a leader who sees him or herself above everyone else. They think more of their self-worth and persona. A leader should work these matters out long before he or she decides to take on the role of leader. Only with secure and accurate self-knowledge and self-awareness is the leader able to establish authenticity, which is important in leading others. A leader who is not honest in self-evaluation tends either to be too tentative or too overbearing to inspire the confidence and trust of those who are working with and under him or her. There is a delicate balance between the two, and a good leader knows when and when not to act.

LISTENING

The last characteristic — and one of the most important — that a leader should have is the ability and willingness to listen. It seems a minor thing, but it is not. So many talented, effective people are not as successful as they could be because they need to develop this skill. Listening is not waiting until the other person is finished talking so you can take the floor. Listening is more than hearing — it is caring about what the other person has to say and using leading questions. A good listener does not pretend to care; he or she actually does. A good leader will have that kind of concern and interest in other people.

Selecting a leader with all of these qualities are the most important factors when building an effective team. Even if those qualities were present in the team itself, without a successful leader, the team would not achieve its greatest potential.

TYPES OF TEAMS

Before you choose which activities to use with your team, it's important to remember what kind of team you're operating. Certain activities may work well with remote teams, younger teams, or teams that see each other every day.

PROJECT TEAMS

These are specific teams created to complete a project. They are usually temporary, only exist while the project is being completed, and are disbanded after the project is completed. A committee created to search for the director of a hospital is an example. The members are from different disciplines in the hospital and have input from their individual departments. Once a director is hired, the committee no longer exists. Even though these teams are temporary, they still can benefit from team building activities. These are usually people who have not worked together before. Rapport building and cooperative play exercises can assist these types of teams to accomplish their goals faster and more efficiently.

The group learns to work together without the pressure of a deadline. Team building activities at the beginning and throughout the team's existence can help keep things fresh and moving. Some of the exercises can help get a stuck team unstuck. The exercises help the team solve problems and become more creative as a group rather than as a collection of individuals.

WORKING TEAMS

These are teams that work together every day with a purpose. The group is more permanent than the project team — although team members may come and go. Their purpose can be flexible. It can be a team that works together every day such as an office unit; a team with one purpose, such as nurses who work in an intensive care unit; or management teams that oversee multiple departments within a company.

VIRTUAL TEAMS

Technology has brought many opportunities into the workforce within the last five years that advance our abilities to get work done. It has also given some of us the opportunity to work from home or telecommute.

According to Global Workplace Analytics, the number of Americans who work from home has increased 103 percent since 2005. The website's research conducted in January 2016 also shows that 2.8 percent of the American workforce telecommutes, which is about 3.7 million employees. But with a large amount of our working population at home, company leaders may find it challenging to get their remote employees to engage in team building activities.

However, the advances in technology make team building sessions accessible for these remote teams. Technology allows us to communicate more efficiently now more than ever. Programs like Skype and FaceTime allow coworkers to communicate face-to-face, which was something unheard of for telecommuters a little over a decade ago. Conference calls also play a part in large-group communication — even for teams who work together every day but have hectic schedules.

Social media also plays a part in effective communication. For example, Facebook now has a feature similar to FaceTime and Skype; and Twitter is a great resource to monitor what stakeholders and the competition are saying about your company's goods and services. These are quick ways to connect with your audience and follow the latest trends. Instagram, Snapchat, and Vine are also great platforms to communicate with coworkers and stakeholders. They are more visual-oriented and can sometimes be more entertaining as opposed to a Facebook or blog post. More platforms are out there for virtual teams to utilize; it's just up to them as to how they wish to communicate with each other and their stakeholders on a daily, weekly, or monthly basis.

WHAT DEFINES TEAM BUILDING?

Sometimes it's easy to forget how important team bonding is for your employees. Trust, communication, and problem solving are just a few major factors that teammates need to experience with each other in order for their team to be successful; and it's just as important for the team leader to push for such behavior.

To portray effective leadership, a team leader needs to be able to build loyalty and choose individuals who fit and work with other team members. Once these building blocks have been established, that's when it's time to choose the best exercises for your team and which areas need to be worked on.

In this book, we have organized the team building activities by specific areas to make it easier for you to pinpoint which ones will work best for your team. Some chapters even have exercises meant for younger employees if your team is new and young.

Different professionals were interviewed for this book to share their experiences in effective teamwork and team building exercises with you; so take advantage of their advice like the examples below:

> Recognize that team building exercises are a critical step. If it is considered a fluff exercise, STOP. Don't proceed, because you will be spending lots of time and money. Senior management must buy into doing constructive team building to solve a real problem. —*Pramod Goel*
>
> Sometimes a team building exercise doesn't work out, and that's okay. Even if the activity turns out not to be entirely successful, the team members will have the common experience and can still learn from it. When an activity isn't successful, then the discussion afterwards becomes the potential learning moment. —*Kim Stinson*
>
> Persons and organizations that do not make the steps necessary toward application after a program will inevitably see little value in future programs.
>
> A successful team building activity requires an equal amount of time in debriefing and evaluating the activity, the outcomes, the effect on the participants, and reinforcing how the results of the activity are relative and critical to the actual industry of those participating.
>
> Many debriefings are disassociated from the participants and do not seem to directly tie into the previous activity. PIT provides a debriefing activity that continues to engage the participants and build on the momentum of the exciting activity portion.

Each pit stop scenario performed by the teams is recorded on DVD for the purpose of immediate improvement feedback, as well as for use during the debriefing. During the debriefing, each participating team has at least one of their recorded pit stops shown in a group setting. While there are many applicable lessons to be learned, the disarming nature and comedic value of non-professionals attempting to perform athletic acts allows a perfect atmosphere for participants to speak openly about their personal experience and feelings. A well-prepared program will leverage this discourse into positive outcomes and additional performance-related sessions. Great times for events are to implement, modify, reinforce, and reward systems that are being utilized to meet the mission of the organization. —*Breon Klopp*

The rest of this book is dedicated to 365 different team building activities. Each chapter addresses the different areas where teams, like yours, may need improvement. In each chapter, the activities are divided up into subcategories to make it easier to search for a specific exercise.

Chapter 1
What to Consider Before Choosing the Right Team Building Activity

Before you pick your activities, your team should decide on a good day to do team building exercises. This can be a casual day in the office or at an office retreat. The time spent on team building exercises will only increase productivity, morale, and teamwork within your organization. If higher administration says they cannot do without you for a whole day, do at least a half-day retreat.

At your planning meeting, decide on a place, time, and other details, such as food. Nothing brings a team together more than eating together. Invite your teammates to bring a dish to the event so they can show off their signature recipes. If your team does not have the room or the time to cook individually, pick a restaurant that the majority of the team can agree on. Plan enough in advance so people can make necessary arrangements. Planning ahead at least two weeks is a good rule of thumb. Decide on a place where you will be comfortable and have plenty of room. It is sometimes a better idea not to have your team building retreat at the place you work — but if time is a factor, then the meeting room will work just fine for most of the exercises in this book. But getting away from the office helps change people's mindsets and allows everyone to relax and be more open and genuine. This is a very important key in effective team building activities.

Here are some venues to consider when you're planning your team building day:

• **A coworker's home**. If it is big and comfortable enough, this can work. Make sure everyone stays afterward to clean and that this is not an imposition on a coworker — just because they have a pool and Jacuzzi does not mean they are obligated to host the team building retreat.

• **A hotel conference room.** You may need to shop around, as this can be a little pricey. However, some places charge by the hour.

• **A restaurant or coffee house conference room.** Make sure there is enough room to move around and do activities. Ask the management if you would be disturbing other customers. Some places may be too loud and distracting, so check out the venue first before making a decision.

• **Libraries.** Public libraries often have rooms you can use that would be large enough to accommodate you and your team. The best thing is that these rooms are usually free. They book up quickly, so plan well in advance.

• **Park picnic shelters.** In many cases, you can reserve a picnic shelter for free. These usually have greater availability during the week. Think of an alternate rain site if you are going to have your team building retreat outdoors.

• **Churches.** These are a great resource and are often free if a team member belongs to the congregation.

• **Clubhouses at apartment complexes.** These are a great place if a member of your team lives at that particular complex. This usually includes access to a pool when the activities are over.

• **Your local YMCA or YWCA.** Usually these organizations have rooms you can use. Again, this is usually only an option if a member of your team has a membership.

Be creative, but plan ahead. Make sure you have an agenda worked out, and give this to team members before the day of the team building retreat. In the agenda, make sure you schedule in breaks and time to eat. Make the dress casual, but encourage people to wear loose clothing because they will be up and moving around.

This is a good opportunity to give members of the team task roles. This gives each team member a sense of being a part of the team, and it also spreads responsibility of planning so the entire project does not rest on your shoulders alone. As the day approaches, check in with your team members to make sure all the preparations are in place.

BEFORE YOU BEGIN A TEAM BUILDING SESSION

As a leader, you probably already know that planning ahead, having a set schedule, and organization are keys to success. But so are to-do lists. Here is a checklist of tasks to complete before you begin each session of team building exercises:

• **Make sure you have enough time for the activities.** If you are racing against the clock, schedule the team building activities for another day. If you rush through an exercise, you are not only wasting time and money, but you are setting the tone for future team building sessions. Team members will not take the activities seriously because you have not made them a priority.

• **Schedule breaks.** You are working with humans not machines. They need breaks to go to the bathroom, and they need a mental break. People have about an hour-long attention span before their minds begin to wander. If you are working with children their attention spans are even shorter.

• **Make sure that you have water and snacks.** People do better when they are hydrated. Avoid sodas and sweet snacks. These can cause some people to fall asleep after a short burst of energy. Fruit and protein foods, like peanut butter, are better and healthier choices.

• **Cater lunch.** If you are doing a daylong team building session, make sure you planned to have lunch brought in. If people leave for lunch, they may be late getting back and they may have discussions about the activities that may be better within the larger group. Some team members can negatively influence others, which kills the whole mood and energy level after lunch. If you have lunch brought in, you can make it a working lunch. You can give team members an assignment after lunch or you can have a group discussion about the activities they have already accomplished. You can also have a guest speaker come in to teach a new team building skill or concept. If they do have lunch on their own, suggest a few places that they can go. Encourage the team members to go in groups to build rapport.

• **Look over the activities you have chosen.** Double check that you have all the supplies you need for each activity. Have a couple back-up activities ready in case you need them. You may have extra time or a particular activity may not work as expected.

• **Look over the space you are using.** Make sure you have everything in place for the activities you have chosen. If you need help setting up, make sure that you have planned this ahead of time. There are a few room setups that work well with these activities.

• **Have tables in a "U" shape.** That way it will give you plenty of room in the middle of the area to do activities. It also allows you to interact with all the team members at once. If you need more room, it is easier to just push tables and chairs backward in this configuration.

• **Have chairs set up in a circle.** In this configuration, everyone is equal and important. It gives a sense that no one is above anyone else and the team is in it together.

• **You may decide not to have chairs in the room.** This is beneficial when you need a larger space to do activities. People can sit in a circle on the floor. Make sure everyone is in optimum health if you choose this configuration, as some people may have difficulty getting up and down. If you choose an outdoor setting, make sure you bring chairs or have each team member bring a chair.

• **No alcohol.** This may seem obvious, but do not allow people to drink alcohol during the team building sessions. Some groups are very close and enjoy socializing. There is a time and place for these sorts of activities, and team building time is not one of them.

- **Accommodating preferences.** If there are smokers in the group, make sure they have a designated place and time to smoke (during breaks).

- **Accommodating people.** Make sure that, if anyone on the team has special needs, accommodations are made ahead of time. Pick activities that are not only age appropriate for your team, but also take into account any member that cannot participate. There are 365 activities in this book to choose from. If a team member is sitting on the sidelines watching, the whole point of team-building can be destroyed.

- **Dress code.** Make sure to tell people to dress in loose, comfortable clothing. Some of the activities can be physically challenging and team members need to dress appropriately. If your organization has a dress code, make sure you get permission for your team to dress down that day.

- **Try to remove any and all distractions.** That means you may have to check in all electronics at the door.

- **Time management.** Make sure team members have cleared their schedules during the time you have scheduled for team building.

- **Rewards.** Consider giving rewards for correct answers to queries and active participation. These can be small candy rewards or some cheap toys to play with like clay or colored pens. They can be motivational rewards like time off from work or a pass to dress down for a day. Rewards can be motivational but at the same time distracting. You are the best judge of your group and how they would react to small prizes and awards.

And before all of this, make sure your team members share goals and a common focus. The team must understand their connection to the larger organization in which they reside. They must understand what it is that their team is supposed to be doing and why the team exists. Once they know what their purpose is they must have a clear understanding of what work they are supposed to be doing and how that work is supposed to be accomplished.

Most teams have a general understanding of why they exist and what they are supposed to do. Good teams go beyond these simple understandings. A good team develops its own ethics and common values. This creates trust among members of the team because they know what is expected of them and that the expectations are the same for everyone else.

The other component of an excellent team is a form of evaluation. This means that, as the team works together, they can continuously evaluate where there are weaknesses and identify and celebrate successes. Once areas are identified that need to be improved, you can use the exercises in this book to help develop strategies and solutions to the areas that need work.

BOOK LAYOUT

Each activity in this book has a number of components to help you set up and play each game. Here are descriptions of each:

1.   **Name of the game:** This describes what the theme of the game is.

2.   **Purpose:** This describes what type of game it is. These can range from getting acquainted to communication and trust games. The purpose describes briefly what the team should get out of the activity.

3.   **Group size:** This describes the right team size for the activity. Too many or not enough people can make a game difficult or impossible to play.

4.   **Level:** This describes how in depth the particular game goes.

   A.   First: This level is a good icebreaker activity used with people who may not know each other or have not worked together very long. These types of activities are usually short and fun. These activities are commonly done as the first activity.

   B.   Basic: This is an activity with a group that has worked together a while. These build basic team building skills. They are used to teach and explore basic principles. These activities do not usually evoke emotional responses.

   C.   Advanced: The team leader should consider this level carefully, as these activities are usually more complex. They deal with more serious issues and can evoke some intense discussion and emotional responses.

These are recommended for groups that have been working together for a while and have done a number of basic exercises because advanced games build upon skills that have already been learned.

5. Materials: This describes what materials are needed to complete the task. It may give suggestions for the area in which the game needs to be played and gives the leader instructions about what do ahead of time to prepare for the activity.

6. Time: This describes how long a game or activity should take. In some cases, it will also give the leader an estimate about how much preparation time is needed.

7. Description: This gives a detailed explanation of the game, how it is played, and what the rules are. It may also contain information about what the team should learn by completing the game. These may include other variations on the game, including advanced level versions of the game.

8. Alternate or Advanced Versions: These require that you look at the original version for guidance. These versions of the exercises need other materials, may create a greater challenge, or may be a more advanced exercise. They are similar but not the same as the original, so read them carefully. These are exercises that add on to more basic versions.

CHAPTER BREAKDOWN

Each chapter has multiple subcategories within it to group similar activities with one another. They are below with their descriptions:

In-House Trainings: These are activities that can be done in the office. If you are tight on funds or time or cannot find a location to hold all of your team members, then these exercises will be beneficial to you.

Company Retreats: These activities are great for team building retreats. Most of them require a decent amount of space or can be performed outside. However, they can be done in smaller spaces or during a meeting; it's up to you as the leader. You know the areas that your team needs to improve on the most; and if one of these exercises is what you're looking for, then find a way to alter it or make it work.

Physical Exercises: These activities require a little more physical activity. None of our exercises require too much work such as sprints or mile runs. It depends on the age of your team members and if they are willing to participate in physical activities.

Creative Exercises: Your employees will be able to put their creative skills to the test in these activities. Most of them are group-related, so employees will put their creative thinking skills together to complete these tasks.

Low Cost with Props: These activities can be done without having to spend an arm and a leg to give your team funs activities to look forward to. Most of them require materials you can find at home or in the office or can be purchased at local dollar stores.

Younger Employees: Not every chapter will have this subcategory, but if you find an activity in this book that you think your younger team would like, then give it a try! Don't feel trapped. You can change these exercises to fit your team and the skills you are trying improve.

As a side note, Chapters 2, 5, 10, and 11 will have different subcategories to fit their topics and the types of exercises included in each.

Chapter 2
Break the Ice: Simple Icebreakers and Exercises for Newly Formed Teams

Icebreakers are the best exercises to introduce new people to one another — especially new team members at an organization or company. Throughout this chapter, there are many icebreaker activities for you to choose from. They are categorized by similarity and concept.

NAME GAMES

1. Who am I (Biography)

Purpose: Getting to know each other

Group Size: 5+

Level: First/Basic

Materials: Index cards, pens for everyone, a list of team members for each player

Time: 10 to 15 minutes (5 to 10 minutes of prep time)

Description: Each person fills out a brief bio form prior to the game. The leader needs to allow about 5 to 10 minutes for team members to fill these out. Include interesting facts about yourself that other members of the group do not know. A leader will hand out the sheet with a list of the members. This list helps the members get to know each other's names and it provides a scratch sheet for the team members to make notes on as the game progresses. The team leader then reads off the number and information on each of the cards. The team members write down on their list who they think it is. The member who is able to accurately identify fellow team members wins.

2. Who am I (Introduce your coworker)

Purpose: Getting to know your team

Group size: 6+

Level: First/Basic

Materials: Paper and pens

Time: 20 minutes

Description: Divide your team up into pairs and give them each paper and pens to complete the activity. Tell them to ask five basic questions about each other and write them down. These questions can vary.

Some examples are:

- What got you into this career field?

- What are your hobbies outside of work?

- What is one fun fact about yourself?

Have the pairs reconvene after 15 to 20 minutes of discussion and tell them to introduce their partners to the rest of the group. This activity is a great icebreaker because it starts personal conversations between new team members.

3. Who am I (TV character)

Purpose: Getting to know each other

Group Size: 3+

Level: First/Basic

Materials: Tape, paper and pens

Time: 5 to 10 minutes

Description: Put the name of a TV character on the back of each member. Each individual will try to determine what TV personality is on his or her back by asking the other team members questions. The person who guesses the name of the character first wins.

4. Who am I (Embarrassing moment)

Purpose: Getting to know each other

Group Size: 5+

Level: First/Basic

Materials: Pens and index cards

Time: 5 to 10 minutes (5 minutes of prep time)

Description: Members are asked to write their most embarrassing moment on index cards and hand them in. The leader should give about five minutes for the team members to write. The leader collects the cards and then reads them off. The members guess whose moment belongs to whom; the one who guesses the most accurately wins.

5. Who am I (Favorite job)

Purpose: Getting to know each other

Group Size: 5+

Level: First/Basic

Materials: Pens and index cards

Time: 5 to 10 minutes (5 minutes of prep time)

Description: Members are asked to write a brief description of the favorite job they have held. The members hand their cards in to the leader. The leader then reads them off. The one who matches the most team members and jobs wins. This exercise can be used as a prequel exercise to further discussion about building a better team.

6. Who am I (Favorite class)

Purpose: Getting to know each other

Group Size: 5+

Level: First/Basic

Materials: Pens and index cards for each team member

Time: 5 to 10 minutes (5 minutes of prep time)

Description: Members write their favorite class in school. This can be from grade school, high school, or college. The members hand in the cards and the leader reads them off. The one who has the most accurate guesses about which class matches which team member wins.

7. The name game

Purpose: An active way to get to know each other

Group Size: 5+

Level: First/Basic

Materials: Nametag stickers and pens. You need enough room to play this game. Chairs and tables should be out of the way.

Time: 5 minutes

Description: Each person writes his or her own name on a tag. The leader then collects all the names and the team sits in a circle. The leader then sticks the tags on the backs of the people at random. When the leader says, "go," everyone gets up and tries to find their tag. Each person also tries to prevent others from seeing the tag that is on their back. When team members find their tags, they grab them, and put them on their chests. The game ends when everyone has found his or her tag.

8. Name that balloon

Purpose: Getting to know each other; learning names

Group Size: 10+

Level: First/Basic

Materials: Balloons, paper and pens

Time: 5 minutes

Description: The team is split up into two or more smaller teams. Each person puts his or her name on a piece of paper, slides the piece of paper into the balloon and then blows it up. A person is chosen to be first in each team. The teams get into small circles and place the balloons in the middle. The selected person chooses a balloon and pops it. He takes the name and calls it out, and the person whose name is called comes and pops another balloon. The rule is that people cannot use their hands or feet to break the balloon. The team that pops all balloons first wins.

9. Getting to know my colleagues

Purpose: Getting to know each other

Group size: 8+

Level: First/Basic

Materials: None

Description: One person starts by shaking the hand of the person to their right. That person responds by repeating the first person's name and their name. The second person shakes the hand of the person to their right and repeats, all around the circle. Encourage silly handshake introductions as long as people say their name.

Then, everyone steps back a half step and is given one a softball. They are to call a name and toss the object to the person whose name is called. The second person says the name of the first person, then names a third and tosses. These repeat until the group gets familiar with each other's names, and then add more balls. Balls should not have to be tossed in any set pattern

10. Speed dating

Purpose: Getting to know each other

Group size: 8+

Level: First/Basic

Materials: Chairs and a timer

Description: Set up as many chairs as you need, for all of your team members, across from one another. Then ask your team members to sit in any chair. They are to get to know each other in an allotted amount of time — usually 2 to 3 minutes is a good time limit. They can ask each other any kinds of questions they want to in that time limit. The group on the right side will stay put when the timer buzzes, and the group on the left will shift over one chair when it buzzes. Choose one side to ask the questions and the other will answer or have them both alternate asking questions.

11. Switch sides if...

Purpose: Team bonding; getting to know your team

Group size: 15 or less

Level: First

Materials: Tape

Time: 20 minutes

Description: Divide a section of the floor with a piece of tape and ask your team to stand on either side of the tape. The team leader will call out statements that the team could relate to easily. If a statement is read that a team player relates to then he or she is to cross over the line on the floor. After every few statements ask your team to talk to the person next to them about a statement they had in common.

This activity is simple, but it gets new teams talking easily. The statements can be related to work, the company, or random, individual preferences that most people would have in common like food, clothing, and TV shows.

12. What are you advertising?

Purpose: Getting to know each other; creative collaborations

Group size: 6+

Level: Basic

Materials: Yarn, poster boards, markers, and stickers

Description: The team leader will punch two holes on each poster. Each team member will get a poster and some yarn. On the poster, team members will put who they are and what they do on the team. They will take the yarn when they are finished and hang the poster around their neck. When everyone is finished, they act as if they are at a party. They mingle and make conversation with each other. They can only talk about what is on their poster or on the poster of the person they are talking to.

13. Human map

Purpose: Getting to know each other

Group size: 4+

Level: Basic

Materials: None

Description: Describe an imaginary map of an appropriate area — it can be national or local — and get your group to visualize it on the floor. Ask them to stand on the part of the map where they currently live. If you are meeting the group for the first time get them to state their name and a unique fact about themselves. You could vary this by asking where people would like to live, go on holiday, or take a vacation.

14. Salt and pepper

Purpose: Getting to know each other

Group size: 10+

Level: Basic

Materials: Paper, tape, and pens

Description: Think of pairs of things such as, salt and pepper, yin and yang, shadow and light, peanut butter and jelly, Mickey and Minnie Mouse, male and female, and so forth. Write each item on a piece of paper — i.e. salt on one piece and pepper on another — and tape one paper on the back of each person making sure they can't see it. When the game starts everyone must walk around asking yes or no questions in order to find out what word they have taped to their backs. Once they figure that out, they need to find their other pair. Learning how to ask the right questions is the key. After the pairs have found each other, have them sit together and learn five interesting facts about each other.

LEARN ABOUT YOUR COLLEAGUES

15. Two truths and a lie

Purpose: Getting to know each other

Group Size: 4+

Level: First/Basic

Materials: Pens and paper

Description: Have your team members get in a circle and give them each a piece of paper and a pen. Tell them to write down two true facts about themselves and one false fact. After they all have finished writing, they will then go around the circle and share their three facts. It's up to the group to try to figure out which fact is a lie for each person who shares. Ask your group to include something unique about themselves that no one would ever guess to be true.

16. 'J' is for jumping jacks

Purpose: Getting to know your team

Group Size: 4+

Level: Basic

Materials: Paper and pens

Time: 20+ minutes

Description: Each team member will break down his or her name by letter. Each letter will represent a word and each word will mean something about that team member. Here is an example for John:

Junior: My father is John Senior

Orchestra: I play the piccolo in an orchestra

Hiking: Hiking is one of my favorite past times

Never: I am always late and never on time for appointments

After they create their names, they must share them with their partners. They can introduce themselves to other members of the group.

Was it easier to learn and remember a person's name this way? Were some of the examples clever? Did you learn new things about your team members?

17. 'J' is for jumping jacks alternate version

Description: In this version, people are paired together. They must share their names with their partners. It's a great way for new team members to get to know one another.

18. Common ground

Purpose: Getting to know your team

Group Size: 6+

Level: Basic

Materials: Paper and pens

Time: 15+ minutes

Description: The group must introduce themselves to other people on the team and make two columns on their paper. The first column contains things they have in common with each other, and the second contains a piece of information that they do not have in common. The person with the most names during a time limit wins.

What do the team members have in common with one another? Were there interesting differences?

19. Color personality tests

Purpose: Getting to know your team on a deeper level

Group size: 4+

Level: Basic

Materials: Exams, answer sheets

Description: Color personality tests are a great resource for both new and old teams to get to know each other better. These tests can be found online along with answer keys. It's usually a survey that asks questions about people's personal preferences and behaviors and, as a result, groups them into a color that represents certain personality traits. It's a great tool to inform your team members about who they are and who their teammates are.

The goal of color personality tests is for teams to get to know whom they relate to and whom they do not so they can work better in the future, and also, so they can know more about themselves.

20. You get one question

Purpose: Team members learn how each other thinks differently

Group Size: 6+

Level: First/Basic

Materials: None

Time: 15 minutes

Description: Think of one scenario that a person would be chosen to take a big step in their life — it could be anything from marriage, leading a new company or commanding an army. Then ask your teams members to think of a question that they consider the perfect question to determine if someone is a perfect fit for the scenario. It can only be one question.

Each person's question reflects their motives and what they think matters to a team. This is a good activity to do before engaging in a conversation about trust, diversity, and leadership. For more of a challenge, you can split them up into pairs for more of a communication exercise also.

Lead a discussion about all the discussions once everyone has shared. Do they agree with the same question or do they disagree? Are there questions than were shared more than once?

21. Answer and ask

Purpose: Team bonding

Group Size: 6+

Level: First/Basic

Materials: None

Time: 10 minutes

Description: Have your group members sit in a circle. Tell them to think of one question to ask the person next to them. Once they have thought of their questions, the game begins. The person chosen to start will ask his or her question to the person next to him or her, then that person will answer the question. But immediately after he or she answers, they need to ask their question to the next person. This keeps going until everyone has asked his or her question.

When that's finished, reverse the way you had them answer and ask their questions in the first round. This time they have to ask the same question but to the person on their opposite side. Then that person has to reply with the answer they said in the first round. It turns into a vocal form of mad-libs. This is a fun game to play as an icebreaker or when you think your team needs an exercise that doesn't require a lot of thinking.

22. Rings

Purpose: Employees will get to know unique or general facts about one another

Group Size: 4+ (in pairs)

Level: First

Materials: No extra materials are needed

Time: 10+ minutes

Description: Have everyone find a partner. One partner is "one" and the other is "two." The "one's" are the inner circle and face outward. The "two's" are the outer circle. They pair up with their partner and face inward. The inner circle asks a question of the outer. The outer circle partners have one minute to answer. The leader says shift, and the out circle moves one person to the left. The same question or a different question can be asked. The same time limit is applied. When everyone in the inner circle has asked everyone in the outer circle a question, it is the outward circle's turn to ask questions. The questions can be about anything, or the leader may state that it needs to be work related. Was this an easy way to meet and get to know people? Was it awkward? Did you wish you had more time with particular people?

23. Life highlights

Purpose: Icebreaker; getting to know your teammates

Group size: 6+

Level: First/Basic

Materials: None

Time: 30 minutes

Description: Ask your team members to close their eyes for one minute and think about the best moments in their lives so far. Tell them it can be anything from personal revelations, marriage, having kids, professional successes, or life adventures. After the one minute is up and they have thought about their life highlights, ask them to keep their eyes closed for another minute and think about 30 seconds of their life that they would want to relive if they only had 30 seconds left to live.

When the second minute is up, go around the room and have each individual share the 30 seconds of their life that they would want to relive and why. This exercise let's your team members reflect back on important moments in their lives and allows them to get to know one another on a more intimate level.

24. I would like you to

Purpose: A creative way for employees to get to know each other; avoiding stereotyping in the future.

Group Size: 6+

Level: First

Materials: Paper, markers and tape

Time: 10+ minutes

Description: Have each person write his or her name on the piece of paper. Tape the paper to the back of the person and have the team mingle with one another for a few minutes. They are to write a word that describes their first impression on the back of the appropriate person. When everyone is finished, the leader has people read each other's backs. They are to introduce the person using the words that were written.

How did the words people used about you make you feel? Were these fair? Are first impressions important?

25. Know your role

Purpose: Creating a positive and supportive environment

Group size: 4+

Level: First/Basic

Materials: Paper and pens

Time: 20 minutes

Description: Give each individual a piece of paper and a pen for this activity. Instruct them to write down nine statements about their new or continuing role in the company. Three of the statements will be three things they want to learn while in this position; the next three are three fears they have about the position, and the last three are three skills they know they bring to the team.

When everyone is finished, have your team members get into small groups to share or have them share aloud with everyone. This exercise creates a positive and supportive environment for the team and gives everyone that extra confidence boost they might need. Encourage others to chime in after someone has shared his or her nine facts. Getting a discussion going about the activity will create your team members to support each other more naturally as opposed to forcing it on them.

26. Rings a bell

Purpose: Getting to know personalities

Group Size: 6+

Level: Basic

Materials: Everyone needs to bring his or her cell-phone

Time: 15 minutes

Description: Ask the group to introduce themselves with some basic information about themselves — name, position, fun fact, etc. As part of their introduction, have each of them play the ringtone they have set as default on their phone. Ask them to explain why they chose that ringtone, even if it's on vibrate, silent, or the general ringtone set for that phone type.

This exercise gives a little insight on your team members' personalities. As the leader, you can ask them more questions about the style of their phone and how much they use it. For example, someone may still have an old flip phone with an antenna. Hearing their explanation for not upgrading or switching carriers could mean they are really relaxed or not crazy about technology, which gives the team more insight about how this person will act on the team.

LOW COST WITH PROPS

27. Sweet stories

Purpose: Getting to know your team

Group size: 4+

Level: Basic

Materials: A large bag of skittles, Smarties, M&M's. or any bag of colorful candy

Time: 20 minutes

Description: Have each team member grab a piece of candy. Make sure you tell them not to eat it just yet. They will share a fact or story about themselves based on the colored candy they picked out in groups. If you want to promote more team bonding, have your team members choose two or three pieces of candy so they can really get to know each other. If they draw the same color two or three times, they still have to share the story based off that color. Below are a few ideas from Venture Team Building that you can assign to each colored candy. Feel free to make up your own, however.

Blue: A time when you felt proud

Green: Name someone you respect and why

Yellow: What are you hoping to achieve by being a part of this team?

Brown: An embarrassing moment

Orange: A time you failed; what did you take away from that experience?

Red: What led you to this job?

Purple: A time you felt really scared

28. Quarter of a century

Purpose: Getting to know your team

Group size: 5+

Level: Basic

Materials: Enough quarters for each team member

Time: 20 minutes

Description: Each person takes a different quarter — you can have fun if you find at least one really old quarter based on the age group of your team. Have the team members introduce themselves to everyone else. They must include something exciting that happened to them or is somehow related to them on the year that is on the quarter they chose.

29. Beach ball toss

Purpose: Getting to know your team

Group size: 5+

Level: Basic

Materials: Beach ball

Time: 20 minutes

Description: Write a series of questions on the beach ball — they can be as complex or simple as you'd like. Have the group stand in a circle and toss the beach ball to one another. When it's caught, they have to introduce themselves with their name and position within the company or team. They also have to answer the question that is written on the ball closest to their right pinky finger. Unlike a regular meeting, this exercise allows your team members to get to know one another in a fun way.

30. True colors

Purpose: Getting to know your team in a creative way

Group Size: 4+

Level: Advanced

Materials: Many different colored markers or crayons

Time: 15+ minutes

Description: The leader picks a different colored marker for each team member. The team members must find someone else that has a similar colored marker. They have 60 seconds to find something they have in common with that person.

31. Picture yourself

Purpose: Creative partnerships; getting to know your team

Group Size: 6+

Level: Basic

Materials: Construction paper, markers and crayons or colored pencils

Time: 20 minutes

Description: Have each team member choose his or her own materials to complete this activity. Give them about 15 minutes to create a drawing that they feel expresses who they are. Once they are finished, pair them up and give them a few minutes to explain their drawing to one another. After they have finished learning about each other's creations, have the entire group get in a circle. Here, each team member will introduce his or her partner and explain his or her drawing to the rest of the group.

This activity gives your employees the opportunity to creatively explain who they are and what makes them tick to the rest of their coworkers. Start a small discussion after about introducing each other this way as opposed to just introducing each other by name.

32. Scavenger hunt

Purpose: Getting to know each other, the company, and how to get around the company. This is a teamwork activity.

Group Size: At least two teams of four

Level: First/Basic

Materials: A list of items around the company. This activity needs to be performed where the team works.

Time: 30+ minutes (prep time depends on how long it takes the leader to go around the company and make a list of items to find)

Description: The leader must go around the building and find different items to add to the list. The list should be no longer than 10 items or you may not see the team members the rest of the day. Items that can be considered:

- Newspaper from six months ago
- Number of employees in the company currently
- Year company was founded
- Board members and their occupations
- Bio of current president
- Where the extra ink cartridges are kept
- Where the copy paper is kept
- Where office supplies are kept
- Hidden items, such as a Pez dispenser (these are placed by team leader; they should be in plain sight)
- Fire evacuation plan drawing
- Fire extinguisher (you can put a number of these to find)

- Number of telephones

- Number of outside doors

- Number of windows

- Mission statement

As a team leader, you can be creative. This is a great orientation exercise because members can find their way around while finding materials and objects they may need while working at the company. Make sure you let other people in the building know that this is going on. Tell team members not to disturb others while they are working. You could do this exercise during lunch hour or after hours.

Divide your members into teams of four. Give each team the list of items to find and a time limit. When time is called, the teams can have a show-and-tell that includes where items were found and the team with the most items wins.

33. The bait and switch hunt

Purpose: Teamwork and competition

Group Size: 6+ (at least two groups)

Level: Basic

Materials: Pencils for each group and paper for each group

Time: 45+ minutes

Description: Each team creates a scavenger hunt list. The rule is that they must be able to find the item themselves. Each team should make a list of at least 10 items. The leader then switches the lists. The leader should give a time limit to find the items and bring them back (or take a picture of the item). The team that finds the most items wins.

34. Resource utilization

Purpose: Employees can learn how their working environment functions in a fun, creative manner.

Group Size: 6+ (2 or more teams)

Level: Basic

Materials: Resources such as phone books, pamphlets, newsletters, magazines, or newspapers

Time: 15+ minutes

Description: The resources are piled in the middle of the room. Each team can send one team member at a time to run and grab a resource. Once the resource is used, it must be returned before another can be used.

The leader shouts out a particular resource, and the teams must try to find it before the other team does.

Here is a list of possible resources:

- Police

- Italian restaurant

- List of local dentists

- Building supplies

- Newspaper wanted ads

The leader may pick resources that team members need to be able to access for their jobs. The team with the most finds wins. This exercise can be done using computers, too, especially if your team members will be working a lot with technology and various computer programs.

GAMES

35. Take what you need

Purpose: A short get-to-know-you activity

Group size: 10+

Level: Basic

Materials: Toilet paper rolls

Time: 30 minutes

Description: Ask the group to sit in a circle. Pass around the toilet paper roll and tell them to take as much as they think they will need (you haven't disclosed what they will need it for just yet). If your employees ask you for what, respond with, "Take as much as you think you will need." Once the roll has been passed all the way around, ask your group to count the number of toilet paper squares they have. Go around the circle and have everyone share a fact or facts about themselves based on the number of toilet paper squares they have. So if they took 10 squares, then they need to share 10 facts about themselves.

This activity is helpful in newly formed teams. It gives everyone the chance to communicate, bond, and get to know one another in timely manner. As the leader, you should jump in the activity so your employees get to know more about you as well.

36. Telephone on paper

Purpose: Getting to know your team; creative communication skills

Group size: 6+

Level: Basic

Materials: Pieces of paper and pens

Time: 20 minutes

Description: Give each team member a piece of paper and tell him or her to draw something simple on it without speaking. Set a time limit and tell them to pass their drawings to the right. Each person will look at the drawing they now have, fold the paper in half and then write what they think the drawing is on top. The paper continues to be passed to the right. Each person reads the description and folds the paper in half to draw what that description said.

When all papers have been returned to the original artist, each member will then reveal what the original drawing was. Have them figure out where things started to go wrong by looking through all the descriptions and drawings on their paper. Encourage a discussion about how important communication is with one another and how easy it is to misunderstand people sometimes, especially on new teams.

37. Group mirror

Purpose: Icebreaker that incorporates communication

Group Size: 6+

Level: Advanced

Materials: No extra materials are needed

Time: 10+ minutes

Description: The team gets into a circle and the team leader randomly assigns each member a number. The teams will then look at one another; team one looks at team two; team two looks at three, and so on. The last number looks at the first number.

The team leader should make sure that everyone knows the person they are looking at. If the person you look at moves, you must make the same exact move. It can be anything from an itch to a cough. The task is for the team to freeze in position for five minutes.

When someone moved, did the person watching him or her blame him or her for not freezing? Did one person's action affect the entire group? Did the group see how easy it was to blame others for their actions?

38. Cake walk

Purpose: Getting to know each other on a time limit

Group Size: 20+

Level: Any

Materials: A music player and an area large enough to move around in. Chairs and tables should be cleared from the playing area.

Time: Five to 15 minutes

Description: The leader calls out various numbers. This will depend on the size of the group. Numbers from two to eight are probably a good range to work in. The leader plays recorded music while the team members talk and interact with one another. The leader stops the music and shouts out a number. The team members then try to get in groups of that number. For instance, if the leader calls out three, then the team members will run and get into groups of three. Whoever is left over must stay outside the playing area. This process is repeated until a small group is left as the winners.

39. Cake walk alternate version

Description: You can use different characteristics along with the numbers.

Following is a list of suggestions:

- Age

- Hair color

- Eye color

- Clothing color

- Shoe color

- Number of children

- Number of years at the company

- Favorite restaurant

- Favorite movie

An example of what the leader might say is: "Groups of three people who are wearing the same color shoes."

This exercise will help members of the group learn more about each other because they have to talk to each other and figure out if they have things in common.

40. Word association

Purpose: Overcoming challenges

Group size: 6+

Level: Basic

Materials: None

Time: 15 minutes

Description: Ask your team to stand or sit in a circle. Pick one person randomly and ask them to say the alphabet in his or her mind. Another person, picked randomly, will ask him or her to stop. The first person must then announce the letter that he or she reached and say a word beginning with that letter. The person who asked them to stop will then say another word that is associated with the first word. To make it more challenging, pick one letter that cannot be used at all. For example, if you pick the letter 'S' then everyone cannot name an associated word that starts with that letter, except for the first person who stopped saying the alphabet on that letter. Anyone who says such a word is disqualified and the game continues. Team members cannot repeat words either. It seems very easy, but it starts to get more challenging as the game goes.

41. Characteristics

Purpose: Getting to know your team

Group size: 10+

Level: Basic

Materials: Paper and pens

Time: 15 minutes (15 minutes of prep time)

Description: Create a bingo board that is 5-by-5 squares. Put information in the squares that would apply to people on the team.

Here are examples:

- Has more than two children

- Has been with the company more than three years

- Owns a red car

Be creative. The better the leader knows the team members the more creative he or she can be. Copy the boards and give them out to the team. Have them ask questions about each other. If the person they are talking to has something in common with a square, have them initial it. The person who has initials first — either diagonally or down — wins. Each person can only initial one space.

YOUNGER EMPLOYEES

42. Who's on base?

Purpose: Getting to know each other

Group Size: 8+

Level: First/Basic

Materials: Bases, or choose items that can be used as bases. The number of bases has to be one less than the number of team members.

Time: 10+ minutes

Description: This is a good icebreaker activity for younger employees. The bases are put into a circle. A team member is chosen as the first person to go. That person stands in the middle of the circle. Everyone has one foot on his or her base. The person in the middle calls out a particular item that he or she is wearing or something that applies to him or herself.

Here are examples:

- White shoes

- Black hair

- Grandchildren

- Drives a truck

- Ate ice cream this week

It can be anything. If what the person in the middle shouts applies to members on their bases, then those members must run and find another base to put their foot on. The person in the middle is also trying to get to one of those bases. One person will be left when everyone is on a base. This person becomes the new caller and must choose something different. The game can continue this way until the leader stops the game.

Chapter 3
Working Together: Team Building Exercises For New And Old Teams

The purpose of this book is to strengthen a team's ability to work together — hence teamwork. This chapter is full of team building exercises to teach your workers how to work together effectively. These exercises promote positivity, support, communication, and problem solving all in one. Choose the best activity that you think your team will benefit from practicing the most.

> For groups new to each other, basic team building activities focused on learning names, interests, and experiences will help form the group. Groups that are well established will also benefit from basic team building activities focusing more on the fun of reconnecting with each other. By observing the interaction of the group during basic activities, the focus can be steered to address specific concerns (communication, leadership, ways of work, etc.) There are team building activities for all types of groups.
> — *Deb Dowling*

IN-HOUSE TRAININGS

43. Can we build it?

Purpose: Teamwork and personal responsibility

Group Size: 4+

Level: Basic

Materials: Building blocks

Time: Five to 10 minutes

Description: The leader builds a small structure out of blocks and has the group analyze it. There is another pile of blocks that contains the same blocks used in the leader's structure. Members choose one block until all of them have been chosen. The rules are that each person may only touch their block and the group must make the same structure as the leader. If a team member touches a block that is not his own, the group must start over again. This exercise emphasizes the importance of personal responsibility for each member on the team, along with patience and teamwork.

44. Can we build it alternate version

Description: After the group has seen the structure the leader covers it back up while team members recreate it. At the end, the leader shows the group the structure again to see how well they did. This version allows team members to lean on each other for support, expand their creative thinking skills, and further test their ability to work under pressure.

45. Team Feud

Purpose: Getting to know your team better

Group size: 6+

Level: Basic

Materials: Questionnaires filled out prior, a desk bell, and either a chalkboard or whiteboard

Time: 20+ minutes (30 minutes of prep time)

Description: This game is similar to the popular TV game show Family Feud. Before you play this game, collect the answers to a questionnaire you have created. Try to get as many people as you can to answer the survey. Tally up the five most popular answers to be used with the game.

Set up a table with the bell. The person who rings the bell first can try to answer the question. Each team should have chairs set up in a line. As each person has a turn, the other members move up a chair and the person who had a turn moves to the back.

Here is the order of play:

1. Two people come up for the challenge.

2. On the white board, make five slots for the correct answers.

3. Ask the survey question. Whoever rings the bell first gets to answer the question first. If correct, you write it down on the board. The two

players sit down at the end of the row on their team's side. You ask the next person the same question.

4.   If the first person rings the bell and does not answer the question correctly, the opposing team gets a chance to answer the question. If the opposing team answers it correctly, then they get to play. If the opposing team does not get it correct, then the other team gets to play.

5.   If the winning team gets three incorrect answers before clearing all the answers on the board, the opposing team gets to offer an answer. If the opposing team is correct, they win. If they answer it wrong, it is a tie. If the winning team gives all five answers before three incorrect answers, they win.

6.   The game is repeated with a new survey question. Whichever team has the most wins is the overall winner.

Here are some sample survey questions:

- What is your favorite color?

- What is your favorite animal?

- What is your favorite place to eat?

- What is your favorite food?

- What is your favorite holiday?

46. Team Feud alternate version

Description: In this version, you ask more in-depth questions that are work or team related.

Here are some examples:

- What is your favorite part of your job?

- What is your least favorite rule at work?

- What is the best part about being a team member?

- What is the team's most shining moment?

- What is the team's funniest moment?

47. Crazy eights

Purpose: Team building, testing memory, and the ability to think quickly

Group Size: 6+

Level: Advanced

Materials: Beanbag and a stopwatch

Time: 20+ minutes

Description: Have the team sit or stand in a circle. Hand the bag to any member and then explain the rules. The first person must throw the beanbag to someone else in the circle. The beanbag cannot go to any person twice. When everyone has had a turn the last person throws the beanbag to the first. Tell the team that they must memorize whom they threw the bag to.

Have the team repeat the design they made and use the watch to see how fast they can do it. Repeat this a couple of times. Get the team to create a strategy to throw faster. Then time them again. Toss in another beanbag for more of a challenge.

Was it important for every team member to work together? Was there a strategy to get the beanbag to move faster?

48. Key people

Purpose: How team leaders and the team can improve basic skills; open communication

Group Size: 9+

Level: Advanced

Materials: Paper and pens

Time: 50+ minutes

Description: Break the team into three small groups. Have the groups identify key people on the team or in the organization. These are people who are essential and that provide necessary support and resources to the team. Give them about five to 10 minutes to complete this.

Have the team come back together and vote on the top three people from the each group's list. This is not a popularity contest; rather, these people hold positions or do work that is essential for others to do their work.

Assign one person to each of the small groups. Read (or give a copy) of the following questions for each group to answer about the key person they have chosen. Give them about 30 minutes to complete the assignment. At the end of the allotted time, have the team reconvene and share what the groups came up with. Allow time for discussion.

- Why is this key person so important?

- What does the key person do for other members of the team?

- What does the key person need from team members to perform his or her job?

- What are the common goals that the team shares with the key person?

- What happens when the team does not work well with the person?

- How can a team member build a positive and successful relationship with the key person?

- What benefit is there to having a positive relationship with the key person?

- What happens when the key person is not available or is missing from work?

- What kind of feedback does the key person give to team members? How can this be improved?

- What kind of feedback are team members giving the key person? How can this be improved?

49. What grade did I get?

Purpose: Team member evaluation

Group Size: 3+

Level: Advanced

Materials: Pens and prepared report cards

Time: 15+ minutes

Description: The leader creates a report card. There should be ten areas that are graded.

Here are some suggestions:

- Works well with others

- Takes initiative

- Helps others

- Does more than their fair share

- Stays late to help

- Arrives early to work

- Has a positive attitude

Each team member grades his or her own card. When they are completed, the team shares their report cards with one another. For a more open activity, have team members pass around their report cards and grade each other. Encourage honesty and truth from your team if you decide to do this version and make sure the activity doesn't become an emotional issue.

How did people's report cards compare with others? Was there an area everyone needed improvement in? Did anyone have any comments they felt were inaccurate on their report card?

50. Conveyor belt

Purpose: Team bonding, communication, and getting to know your team

Group size: 10+

Materials: Tape

Time: One minute for each person; five to10 minutes for explanation

Description: Ask everyone to stand in two lines facing each other along the tape. Everyone should place his or her hands on the shoulders on the person across from him or her. They are now partners.

You should not get in the line but actively watch and instruct the activity. This is a complicated exercise to lead, and timing and talking is really challenging.

If there is:

- An odd number of people, ask the person without a partner to stand next to you.

- An even number of people, ask one pair to step out of the line and stand next to you. They can play the next round.

Ask the partners to introduce themselves to one another. Now explain that you are going to read a series of questions. The person on the side of the line to the left of you will always answer the question first. When you yell "switch" the person to the right of the line will have a chance to answer.

It starts to get complicated because after three rounds you will have the people on the left side ask the question to the person to the right of their partner. They are still connected to their original partner though. See how long your team can do this activity before members start to get frustrated.

COMPANY RETREATS

51. Forefathers

Purpose: Diversity and acceptance

Group Size: 4+

Level: Advanced

Materials: Paper, pens, colored markers or pencils

Time: 30+ minutes

Description: The team leader reads the following scenario to the team:

"You have just been notified that you inherited a parcel of land near Alaska. According to the maps, it does not belong to any country and, therefore, is a

country unto itself. It is up to the team to create a country from scratch."
Here are the tasks that need to be accomplished. They may take more than one session to complete, so split up the tasks so that they can fit into your time frame.

- Country name

- Constitution

- Language of inhabitants

- Monetary system

- System of government

- Branches of government

- Voting

- Main commodity

- Culture

- Religion

- Military

- Political standing with other countries

- Country bird or flower

Lead a discussion after each team has presented their new country about diversity and acceptance. How did team members work together and put aside personal beliefs for this exercise? Were there any arguments? Why is this conversation important?

52. Horse show

Purpose: Creativity, listening, trust and building your team

Group Size: 8+ (enough for four teams)

Level: Advanced

Materials: Small items that can be used to create four small obstacle courses. These can be cones, balls, ropes, Frisbees, or anything else. You need a large area to create four obstacle courses.

Time: 30+ minutes

Description: There are four groups that must create simple courses in an assigned area. This can be areas within a department or multiple areas around the company. When teams have finished, they will present their obstacle course to the others. Each team learns about the other team's course and gets directions to complete it.

From there, those who didn't create the course will compete in it — one team against another like a relay race. If anyone messes up, they must go to the back of the line to try again.

Did everyone complete it the first time through? Did people learn from other people's mistakes? Did people give clear instructions? Did we learn anything new about the department the obstacle course was made in?

53. Fearless Factor

Purpose: Teamwork, trust, patience, and creativity

Group Size: 6+ (at least two teams)

Level: Advanced

Materials: This depends on the challenges that are set by the teams. Try to limit the materials to items that are nearby. You do need pen and paper for each team.

Time: 30+ minutes

Description: Each team must come up with six challenges that they can accomplish and win. The team coming up with the challenge must be able to do the challenge before they can add it to the list for another group to accomplish. Here are some categories of possible challenges:

- Physical challenges. These are challenges that the group can do as a group such as each member jumping rope ten times without tripping or stopping.

- Non-physical challenges according to who is in your group. An example is that everyone can sing the happy birthday song in Spanish.

- Gross challenges (like the game show Fear Factor). Do not make the activities too gross or people might get sick. This one will take some pre-planning. You can do things such as eating ice cream with mustard and ketchup.

The groups hand in their lists. The leader calls out a challenge and the team that created it must be able to demonstrate it. The challenges cannot be something that no other team can do. The other teams have the chance to do the challenge. If they can successfully do it, they get a point. The leader goes through all of the challenges. The team with the most points wins.

Discuss with the team how they came up with the challenges. How did the group cooperate to accomplish the challenge? Did the group members rely on the other people in their group to meet the challenge? Did they feel confident in their other team members for various challenges? Did some people have special talents that others did not?

54. Team mall

Purpose: Highlight individual strengths; creative thinking

Group Size: 4+

Level: Advanced

Materials: A piece of butcher paper for each team member, paints, brushes, water and newspaper

Time: 45+ minutes (30+ minutes of prep and clean up time)

Description: Each team member will create a storefront in the Team Mall. The store should represent them. It should contain items that represent their positive aspects and skills. They are to paint the storefront full size. The paint should dry and then the room will be turned into the Team Mall as all of the storefronts are hung up. Each team member should explain his or her store.

How did team members decide what their stores would be? How did team members feel when the mall was constructed? Did the mall feel drab or exciting? Did others encourage their coworkers after each storefront was presented?

55. The emotional bus

Purpose: Learning to express emotions

Group Size: 6+ (in pairs)

Level: Advanced

Materials: Two chairs and paper slips

Time: 20+ minutes

Description: The leader should write down different emotions on slips of paper. The first pair comes, and each person selects an emotion but does

not share it with anyone. The pair has three minutes to act out a scene, each of them using the emotion they are given. The leader or another team member may pick the scenario. For example, a common scenario is when two people wait for a bus.

When they are finished, the rest of the team can guess what the two emotions are. The next pair goes, and the procedure is repeated. This activity will help team members become more comfortable with each other and open to emotional conversations in the future.

Was it hard to act out an emotion? Was it hard to guess other people's emotions? Did anyone struggle with this activity?

56. What's your fortune?

Purpose: Getting to know your team; creating an open conversation with your team

Group Size: 4+

Level: Basic

Materials: Fortune cookies

Time: 20+ minutes (60 minutes of prep time if you make the cookies)

Description: What better way to build a team than to bake cookies together? Look for any cookie recipe online to complete this task as basic or challenging as you wish. You'll add your own fortunes and positive affirmations in these cookies for the group to answer. You may also ask them questions about the future of the group. When the person opens the cookie, they must answer the question.

Here are some examples:

• What was your favorite activity with the team?

• What is your hope for the team in the future?

- How would you describe the team's function to someone?

- Why are you glad to be on the team?

- Where do you see the team in five years?

Keep the questions light and fun. This can be used as a celebration or final activity for a longer team building session.

57. What is it?

Purpose: Teamwork

Group Size: 4+

Level: Advanced

Materials: Pen, paper, five similar objects (like a tennis ball, softball, baseball, etc.)

Time: 10+ minutes

Description: Have the team members pick an item from the five. They must draw a picture of the item with their non-dominant hand. When they are finished, have each member show his or her picture. The team will vote on which object they think it is. The one with the most right guesses wins.

You can do this exercise with any inanimate objects such as things around the office or materials you need for a project.

How did it feel to do a simple task differently? Was it frustrating? How did it feel when people did not recognize what you drew?

58. Four square

Purpose: Getting to know each other

Group Size: 15+

Level: First/Basic

Materials: A large room broken up into four squares with a number marked in each, tape, dice (or a similar method to randomly pick numbers), and a list of 20 questions and four different answers

Time: 10 to 15 minutes (prep time 10 to 15 minutes)

Description: The leader divides and marks the room ahead of time. The leader will have a sheet of questions and four possible answers.

Here is an example:

What flavor of ice cream do you like?

1. Vanilla

2. Chocolate

3. Strawberry

4. Cookie Dough

When the question and answers are read, then the members find which square fits their answer. The leader then picks a number by rolling a die or similar method (the number should be one through four). Whatever number is picked, those team members must sit down. The game is played until only a couple of people remain.

PHYSICAL EXERCISES

59. Team bocce ball

Purpose: Teamwork; let off some steam

Group Size: 6+ in at least two teams

Level: Basic

What do you need? A two-liter bottle filled with water, small balls, and cones or objects to mark off the playing area

How much time does it take? 10+ minutes (10 minutes of prep time)

Description: The area is marked off with four cones or objects; 30-by-30 feet is a good size. The bottle is placed in the middle. The teams surround the area. The goal is to get a ball to touch the bottle but not to knock it over.

Here are the rules:

- The players may never enter the playing area

- The balls can be thrown at anytime

- A ball may be hit with another ball to knock it away from the bottle

- A ball may be knocked out of the playing area and reused

- If the bottle is knocked over, the team that does it loses three points

- The game ends when no more balls can be used

- The team with the most points wins

- Each team is given the same number of balls at the beginning of the game

- If a person enters the play area, his team loses two points

The leader is the scorekeeper. Discuss how it felt for other team members to compete against you. Did everyone score? How did it feel to get a ball knocked away from the goal? Did other team members help you score?

60. Team race

Purpose: Communication

Group Size: 4+

Level: Basic

Materials: A start and a finish line. These can be ropes or tape.

Time: 10 minutes

Description: Place the start and finish line about 20 feet from one another. The task is simple. The team must begin at the starting line and finish exactly together. If they do not pass the line together, they must start over. This is much harder than it seems. The leader is the judge of whether they accomplished the task.

Was this a hard task? What were the problems that arose? Was there a problem in communication?

61. Use your Feet

Purpose: Teamwork

Group size: 6+

Level: First

Materials: Exercise ball or any large weightless ball

Time: 20 minutes

Description: Get all of your team members to lay on their backs with their legs resting against a wall. Put the ball you chose for this activity in between or on top of an end person's legs. The goal is for the team to pass the ball, without dropping it, to one another using only their legs. If the ball falls, then they have to start all over.

If you have a large team, you can turn this activity into a fun competition. Split the group up into equal teams and time them to see which teams completes the task the fastest. You can offer prizes to make them more excited; items like work supplies, gift cards, or coupons would motivate them to participate in this activity.

62. Dodge-mallow

Purpose: Team rapport; let off some steam

Group Size: 4+ broken up into two groups

Level: First/Basic

Materials: A bag of marshmallows (regular size, not minis unless you want to make it harder), an area large enough to play and tape. Divide the playing area in half with tape.

Time: 5+ minutes

Description: This is a great game to start off a team building session or to liven things up when things are getting boring. This is based on the game dodge ball except you are using marshmallows instead of balls. Give each side a few marshmallows and tell them to start.

Each side tries to hit the other side's players with the marshmallows. If they get hit they must leave the playing area. If a member of their team catches a marshmallow then a member on the sideline may return. The games ends when an entire team is eliminated. You can either divide the teams up yourself or let them pick their teams.

63. Fitness test

Purpose: Teamwork, team support and physical activity

Group Size: 6+ (two teams)

Level: Advanced

Materials: Balls of various sizes, hula-hoop, jump rope, or any other item that can be used in a physical challenge

Time: 60+ minutes (20+ minutes of prep time)

Description: This exercise is best performed outdoors. The goal is for one team to reach 50 points first. You can assign various points to complete different tasks using the items available. You might have some team members be referees. That way, a few different activities can be going on at the same time. Each team will be provided with a list of possible physical challenges. The points are not assigned for just the completion of the exercise, rather for the level of enthusiasm and cheering for the person completing the challenge. Do not let the group know this until they have begun some of the exercises.

How did it feel to be awarded points for your cheering section? Did the feeling of the challenges change when the teams were awarded points for cheering? Did it make completing the challenges more fun?

CREATIVE EXERCISES

64. Improvisations

Purpose: Teamwork

Group Size: 3+

Level: Basic/Advanced

Materials: Paper with different problems or disasters that could occur within the organization. The team leader needs to write them down on folded slips of paper.

Time: 20 to 30 minutes (10 minutes prep)

Description: Improvisations can be a great way to get everyone laughing or brainstorming about a particular situation. It is hard, though, for people to come up with situations and characters off the tops of their heads, particularly if they are feeling self- conscious. As the team leader, you should think of a situation that could happen at work and the characters that would be involved in it. Relate the situation to the company and then write each character on a piece of paper.

After you have written all your characters, have your team pull them out of a hat or bowl. Have them visualize what is on their piece of paper. Ask them to think about how they would handle this situation or what the protocol would be for this situation along with the role they are going to be acting out with everyone else.

After a few minutes, tell them they all have to improve the situation together. The goal is for them to figure whom each other is and what situation they are dealing with — kind of like charades. However, do not let them discuss and plan before getting up to do it. This means that they each need to communicate silently during the improvisation to determine the situation and work together to get everyone to safety (depending on the scenario you chose). The leader should give them a time limit to play out the scene. Split your team up into smaller groups if you have a large number or people. Give them different situations if you decide to do the activity this way. It will be more fun for the audience to try to figure what their peers are trying to portray.

65. Comic strip

Purpose: Preparation, creative thinking and getting to know each other

Group Size: 4+

Level: Basic

Materials: Comic strips, an overhead projector and screen (optional), transparencies (optional). Whiteout the talk bubbles above the characters' heads. Make copies and transparencies if you like. Have a different comic for each small group of two to three people.

Time: 10 to 15 minutes (20 to 30 prep time)

Description: Each team fills in the bubbles on their comic strip. The team decides what is said. If you are using transparencies, make sure the teams fill it out to share. After they finish, have them share their strips and why they chose what they said in their comic strips.

In another version the team leader picks themes, emotions, or specific situations that the characters are faced with in the comics. You can use this exercise to prepare team members for unplanned situations in the workplace and also introduce them to their teammates.

66. Big picture

Purpose: Communication

Group Size: 4+

Level: Advanced

Materials: A large poster board or foam-core board, colored pens or pencils

Time: 20+ minutes (10 minutes of prep time)

Description: The leader cuts the board like large puzzle pieces so that each team member has his or her own piece. The leader will tell the teams to draw a picture that they think represents a piece of the team.

The goal is for the group to draw one large picture when the pieces are put back together. Allow 15 minutes to complete their pieces. When they are finished, put the puzzle together to see how the picture turned out.

Discuss why communication between team members was so important to complete the picture. How did they decide what to draw? Did one person direct the others? How did members feel about working with others to create something bigger? How did it feel to have their piece fit?

67. Team war

Purpose: Learning to deal with change

Group Size: 6+ (two teams)

Level: Advanced

Materials: No extra materials are needed

Time: 20+ minutes

Description: The team is split up into two groups. The leader will take a team member from each group. Those two will be given an object that they must allow a group to guess. They are to go from group to group and answer only yes or no questions. The team that guesses the object first wins the round. They then yell "bingo." Both team members that played must go to the winning team. The next round begins with two different members, and they repeat the same process with different objects. The game is won when all employees are on the same team or there is a tie between two teams.

The purpose of this activity is to get your employees to adapt to change and work with people they never have before. Ask was this game hard to play? Did it take a different kind of strategy? What was it like to work with people you weren't used to?

68. Group timeline

Purpose: Getting to know your team visually and culturally

Group size: 4+

Level: First

Materials: A bulletin board, thumbtacks, pens and paper

Time: On-going

Description: Purchase a large bulletin board or push board for your team and create a blank timeline. The first date on the timeline can be when your oldest team member was born or when the company was founded. Also include important dates for the company (i.e. changing names, merging with another company, launching a new product) whatever made your company what it is today. Next, have your team members take four slips of paper and write down four important moments of their lives. They are to pin them to the timeline when it occurred.

This exercise will help your team members see each other in a more visual, positive way. It will help them understand cultural and generational differences and how important those aspects are to the team's success. It's also a more fun, creative way for them to get to know more about each other.

LOW COST WITH PROPS

69. Cookie towers

Purpose: Creative thinking, breaking away from work and teamwork

Group Size: 4+ (two or more teams)

Level: First/Basic

Materials: Sandwich-style cookies. Each team is given the same number of cookies.

Time: Five to 10 minutes

Description: Divide your participants into groups of four to six. Each group is given the same number of sandwich-style cookies. The goal is to create the tallest tower of cookies that stands for a specific time period.

70. The plastic cup pyramid

Purpose: Teamwork and communication

Group size: Groups of six

Level: First/Basic

Materials: One rubber band per group, six 3-foot pieces of string per group, six plastic drink cups per group, and a table for each group

Time: 20 minutes (10 minutes of prep time)

Description: Tie one end of the six strings to each rubber band. What you will have is a circle (rubber band) with six spokes or rays coming from it. Places the cup face down on the table. Each team is given a rubber band with strings on it and each member holds one string (or two if there are less than six members). The challenge is to use the rubber band to pick up the cups and build a pyramid. You cannot use your hands to touch the cups even if they fall onto the floor. The team that can build a pyramid first wins. If you do not have enough to make two teams you can have your team just do it as a single challenge.

71. The great hunt purpose

Purpose: Teamwork; introducing your team to the company

Group Size: 4+ (you need pairs or larger groups for this activity)

Level: First/Basic

Materials: Bags. This activity takes place at the company or an area where items can be collected.

Time: 30+ minutes

Description: Each team is given a bag. They are instructed to gather items that begin with different letters of the company's name. For example: If your company were named "The Fried Fish Company," you would need to find items that begin with the following letters. Some letters you would have to find more than one item for.

F = 2 items	R = 1 item	I = 2 items	E = 2 items	D= 2 items
S =1 item	T = 1 item	C = 1 item	O = 1 item	M = 1 item
P= 1 item	H = 2 items	A = 1 item	N = 1 item	Y = 1 item

That is a total of 19 items. For example, for "P" you might collect a pencil.

There should be a time limit on the activity. Whoever can bring back the most items in the allotted time wins. You may want to set rules about disturbing others.

Chapter 4
Collaboration Activities For Teams From Different Departments

A collaborative team can mean a couple of different things. It can be people from completely different departments working together for the first time, despite how long they have been with the company, or it can mean a collaborative environment where all team members work together to succeed.

The U.S. Office of Performance Management says collaboration is essential to any team's success. Officials suggest team members practice the following to create a collaborative environment in their workplace:

- Have a common purpose and goal

- Trust each other

- Clarify roles

- Communicate openly and effectively

- Appreciate diversity

- Balance the team's focus

The activities in this chapter, as well as throughout the book, focus on all of these suggestions. Each exercise will teach your team the importance of collaboration and working together.

IN-HOUSE TRAININGS

72. Team slogan

Purpose: The perfect exercise to get new team members acquainted with one another and their preferences, especially if they are from different departments.

Group Size: 4+

Level: Basic

Materials: Paper, pencils and a list of company slogans

Time: 20+ minutes (10 minutes of prep time)

Description: Begin the discussion by talking about different companies and their slogans. Give the team some examples you have selected. Have members pick a famous slogan that they think fits the team. Have the members share their responses and why they chose a particular slogan.

73. Team slogan alternate version

Purpose: In this version, teammates can get their creative juices flowing

Group Size: 4+

Level: Advanced

Materials: Paper, pencils, and a list of company slogans

Time: 20+ minutes (10 minutes of prep time)

Description: After you complete the first exercise, have the team brainstorm to create its own team slogan. Begin by having team members list nouns, verbs, adverbs, and adjectives that represent the team.

Here is a sample list:

- Fast

- Intelligent

- Comical

- Diverse

- Determined

- Quickly

Now have each team member use words from that list to create one sentence that captures the essence of the group. Have the team members share their slogans. Vote to see which is best. Write or print out the selection and post it for the team to see and enjoy.

Note: Some team members may be better at word smithing than others. That is fine just keep things moving. In the end, everyone will vote about the final product.

74. Create your own game

Purpose: Team collaboration and creative thinking

Group size: 10+

Level: Basic/Advanced

Materials: Paper and pens (random supplies if you wish)

Time: 45 minutes

Description: This is a simple exercise that you can use to build creative thinking, communication, and collaboration among your team members. Split your team up into multiple groups, no less than four, and tell them to come up with their own game. If you want to provide random supplies, then you can, but it's not necessary. The groups can write out their game its description and rules on a piece of paper. Give them 45 minutes to complete the task. Have each group present their game at the end and demonstrate it if possible.

75. Common book

Purpose: Creativity, collaboration, and recollection

Group size: 4+

Level: Basic

Materials: One large scrapbook, pens, tape and scissors

Time: On-going

Description: This exercise is a team building activity that will take place over time rather than in just one sitting. Put a large, blank scrapbook in a space that is accessible to everyone. It will be used for team members to write down encouraging quotes or reminders, add pictures or stories from memorable times at work, and whatever else you and your team think would be beneficial for everyone to remember.

The book can be used for as long as you think necessary — a couple months, a year or as long as it takes for the team to complete a large project. When the time limit is up, save the scrapbook and put out a new one. Encourage the team to fill up the book before time runs out. This will be a great resource for team members to utilize if they ever feel discouraged while working.

76. Ideas on building blocks

Purpose: Brainstorming and valuing ideas

Group size: 4+

Level: Basic

Materials: Large sheets of paper and pens

Time: 30 minutes

Description: Create fictional problem that your team members have to solve. It can be anything your company could face at any time — a new product malfunction, brainteaser, riddle, or design challenge — basically anything that needs a solution. Have your team sit in a circle and write down a solution that they think will help solve the problem. They only need to write a couple sentences. Start with one person and then have them pass the paper around the circle until everyone has had a chance to answer.

You can continue for several rounds to get more feedback. Once creative juices start flowing it may be difficult to get your team to stop thinking. Go over all of the solutions together and discuss which ones would work more than others. Make sure it's a problem that you would know how to handle.

This exercise shows the value of everyone's ideas no matter personality type. It forces everyone to participate because everyone gets a turn or two instead of a few people running the show.

COMPANY RETREATS

77. Cross-country skiing

Purpose: Teamwork

Group Size: 4+ divided into two teams

Level: First/Basic

Materials: Two boards, 8 feet in length and about four inches wide, different colored cloth strips (they can be bandanas or about that size), large enough area to ski across

Time: 15 to 25 minutes

Description: You give each team two boards or skis and the cloths. You can make the cloths different colors for each team. The rules are that up to half the team may move across the room at a time. They may not slide the skis and they cannot touch the skis with their hands. The first team to get all their members to the other side wins. They must bring the skis back across the snow to pick up more team members.

Note: There is a trick to this. If the team thinks about it they can tie their feet to the skis with the cloth. This takes teamwork and team thinking.

78. The big tournament

Purpose: Teamwork

Group Size: 12+ (multiple teams)

Level: Advanced

Materials: Materials needed depend on the exercises chosen, paper and pencil for the judges

Time: 2+ hours (30+ minutes of prep time)

Description: This is a multi-exercise challenge. Your team will compete with other teams for a prize. Each team must choose a team leader. These leaders then switch teams and become the team judges.

Before the tournament, the leader must choose a list of challenges. These can be chosen from other exercises in this book. The exercise is designed to create healthy competition to see if your team has been learning from the team building exercises and can put what they learned into practice.

Each team has the same list of challenges and can pick any one they want. The judges decide whether or not the challenges were completed. The team with the most challenges completed wins. You can set a time limit of two hours or you can make it a daylong event. Each team leader should have a discussion with their team.

Discuss what it felt like working as a team against others. Did the challenge make the teamwork better or worse? Were some team members highly competitive? Were some team leaders left out? How did it feel to win or lose the tournament? Did the team members feel a sense of pride in being a part of the team?

79. Build a raft

Purpose: Teamwork; promoting positivity

Group Size: 10 to 30+

Level: Basic/Advanced

Materials: Supplies to build a raft (cardboard, box cutters, PVC pipe, and duct tape)

Time: 45 minutes (15 minutes of prep and explanation)

Description: This activity works best if you have multiple retuning group members as well as new ones. Tell your group they will be split up into smaller groups and they will have 45 minutes to build a raft that can float on water with a person on top or inside it.

The catch is returning group members are not allowed to help. Instead, they will either be really negative, disengaged, or rude during the entire 45 minutes. Observe how new team members react to the veterans' attitudes and be sure to share positive thoughts at the end. Tell the veterans what "attitude" they are to portray during the exercise in private so new members don't catch onto the game.

The point of this exercise is show that not every member is always going to be engaged, helpful, or even happy to be at work that day. But as a team, it's important to figure out how to handle these situations and personalities when responsibilities start to pile high.

Lead a discussion afterwards about how certain group members handled the veterans: Did they try to include them? Or did they ignore them altogether? Were rude comments made in return?

As a side note, this activity is done best at a company retreat near water. However, you can change it to fit your company's requirements as needed.

80. Grab-bag skits

Purpose: Energizing your team

Group size: 10 to 50

Level: Basic/Advanced

Materials: Bags and random objects that can be used as props in scenes

Time: 30 minutes

Description: Form groups of three to eight people or how many ever you need for the activity to run smoothly. Give each group a bag with six random objects in it. The groups are to create a three-minute skit using all the props in their bag. You can either assign your groups a general topic to act out or make up their own skits. Give them five minutes to figure out what they are doing. Each team member has to participate. At the end, pick which group you felt performed the best and give them a prize. This exercise encourages others to step out of their comfort zone and have a little bit of fun while they are at work.

81. Mouse trap

Purpose: This exercise is great practice to show your team that everyone from a different department has something to contribute to a project.

Group Size: 6+ in at least two teams

Level: Advanced

Materials: Items to make a machine.

These are small items such as:

- Marbles

- Scissors

- Paper

- Toilet paper rolls

- Sticks

- Silverware

Time: 20+ minutes

Description: This exercise is based on the childhood game "mouse trap." The teams should use the items provided to create a machine that, once set in motion, will continue to work without human interaction. For instance a marble could hit a pencil that falls and hits another ball. The team that can create a "mouse trap" that works the longest wins. Have each group present its mousetrap to the others.

Discuss with the group how they worked together. Did some people do the work while others were on-lookers? Was everyone a part of the process? Did some people bring special skills to the task?

82. Mouse trap alternate version

Purpose: Expand collaborative and teamwork behavior further

Description: In this version, have each group help the other improve their machine. How did it feel to have others improve your design? Did you feel defensive about their improvements?

PHYSICAL EXERCISES

83. Untying the knot

Purpose: Cooperation and teamwork

Group Size: Eight to 10 people (you can split this activity into groups for a competition)

Level: First/Basic

Materials: No materials except a large enough area to move around in. This is a great outdoor activity.

Time: 5 to 10 minutes

Description: The team gets into a circle. Each members grabs the hand of someone else but never two hands from the same person. Then look at the group; everyone will be in a large knot. The challenge is to untangle without anyone letting go of hands. They can step over, under, twist, or do anything to return to a large circle again. This can be very challenging, but a lot of fun. You will see the leaders come out in the group as they tell the others what to do next.

84. Double Jeopardy Ping-Pong

Purpose: Getting to know each other, rapport building and teamwork

Group Size: At least two teams of two

LEVEL: FIRST/BASIC

Materials: Ping-Pong table, four Ping-Pong paddles, one or two Ping-Pong balls. You also need enough room to play the game. You can go to a game room or set up your own tables.

Time: 10 to 20 minutes (prep time involves setting up the table and making sure that there is nothing around that could get broken)

Description: In this activity, you run Ping-Pong doubles tournaments in which partners have their right and left hand bound together. This promotes teamwork and breaks down barriers. As a leader you might consider putting pairs together who usually do not work together.

85. Triangulate your space

Purpose: Team exercise

Group size: 10+

Level: Basic

Materials: None

Time: 20 minutes

Description: Assemble your team into a triangle; they should be standing side-by-side and facing inward. Leave one person out of the triangle and put them in the center of the shape — he or she is the spinner. You will spin him or her in a small circle while the triangle shifts for a short period of time. The triangle people can either condense or expand their shape as much as they want but without switching spots with the person next to them. After you call time, the spinner will have to remember whom he or she was facing and in what direction before the triangle shifted.

This activity is just a fun way to get the blood pumping and take a small break from work-related responsibilities.

CREATIVE EXERCISES

86. Classify this

Purpose: Teamwork and creative thinking

Group size: 10+

Level: Basic

Materials: 20 random objects, paper and pens

Time: 20 minutes

Description: Break your team into small groups and give them each a piece of paper and a pen. Have all groups circle around a large table with 20 random objects of your choosing on top of it. The broader the objects are the more creative your team will have to think. For example, you can include jewelry, kitchen and office supplies, pet toys, or anything that comes to your mind.

Tell your teams that they are to classify all of the objects on the table into four groups. They can be whatever four classifications they wish. Give them 10 minutes to complete the task and make sure other teams are not listening in on another. The classification systems should be dramatically different. This exercise encourages your team to rethink how they view everyday objects and forces them to see commonalities among objects that they would not have noticed before. This can lead into a discussion about to solve problems with solutions that do not seem related but, if they looked a little closer, they might be.

87. Build a car

Purpose: Creating team identity and improving collaborative thinking

Group Size: 4+

Level: Basic

Materials: A dry-erase board or a flipchart

Time: 10+ minutes

Description: The leader will draw the outline of a car on the chart. The team members must add parts of the car. The car part must relate to the team. An example is a window so team members can communicate clearly.

Was it hard to build a car based on parts of the team? Did everyone participate? Was the car large or small? Was the car fast or slow? Did the car need work or was it missing anything?

88. Spot it

Purpose: Energize your team

Group size: 10 to 20

Level: Basic

Materials: None except what each team member wore to work that day

Time: 20 minutes

Description: Assemble your team into two lines facing each other. One line will turn around and the other will have 40 seconds to change 10 things about their appearance. It can be jewelry, untied shoelaces, an un-tucked shirt, or anything they can think of. After the 40 seconds is up, the other team will turn around and try to distinguish what is different about the person standing across from them. Once each pair has identified all the changes, then each group switches and the other line gets to change 10 things about their appearance. This activity helps with memory and brain stimulations; it's a good exercise to do if your team is feeling tired or unmotivated.

LOW COST WITH PROPS

89. Mummy wrap

Purpose: Rapport and creative collaboration
Group Size: 6+ broken into two teams or more

Level: Basic

Materials: Toilet paper

Time: 10+ minutes

Description: A person is chosen to be the mummy, and they are wrapped in toilet paper. They may be decorated any way the team chooses, such as a lighthouse, a famous movie character, or anything else that comes to mind. When they are complete they can be shown off to the other teams. Make sure you have a camera ready.

This is an exercise to do for fun to take a break from a hectic day, week or month. This type of activity is also better to do at a company retreat.

90. Mummy wrap alternate version

Purpose: Rapport and creative collaboration

Description: Choose the object or character for the teams — something relate to a project, the team, or the company, for example. The team that does the best job (judged by you) wins. This gets teams to be creative and work together with a common goal in mind.

91. Spaghetti and gummy bears

Purpose: Creative collaboration and team competition

Group size: 16 to 28

Level: Basic/Advanced

Materials: Dry spaghetti noodles and multiple bags of gummy bears

Time: 15 minutes

Description: Separate your team into four groups. Give them each a pack of dry spaghetti noodles and gummy bears. They are to build a tower only using those two items. Whichever team has the tallest spaghetti-gummy-bear tower and can stand for three minutes without falling apart wins. If it falls before the 3 minutes us up, then that team loses. This exercise is a fun activity to do to promote teamwork, communication and creative thinking.

92. Build your team's house

Purpose: Team building and creative thinking

Group Size: 4+ (if the group is too large, break into smaller groups)

Level: Advanced

Materials: A gingerbread house kit (these can be found during most holidays), a food color pen or colored frosting tube

Time: 20+ minutes

Description: Have the team build the house out of the materials you purchased. Make sure that, as they are building, they are including each member's name in the house. The names should be placed in reference to how they fit into the team. For example, a person may have his name on the wall if he is a good support.

When the team is finished, they can display their house. They are to explain why they chose to put names in certain places. This can be displayed for the holidays at the office or, better yet, bring out napkins and let them eat it.

93. Mouse in a pipe

Purpose: Collaborative communication

Group Size: 4+

Level: Basic

Materials: One marble, a small length of pipe for each team member and a cup

Time: 20+ minutes

Description: Place the cup on the opposite side of the room from the team. The task is to get the marble to the cup by using only the pipes. They cannot touch the marble, and the marble cannot fall or they have to start over again. They cannot move while the marble is in their pipe. Once the marble leaves their pipe they can walk again.

Give the team a few minutes to come up with a plan that they think will work best for this exercise. They can use their pipes in any way they think will work best.

Chapter 5
Team Bonding: Activities to Make Your Teams Stronger

After working at an organization for a period of time, it's normal to develop relationships with your employees and coworkers; they may or may not become some of your closest friends. In that case, a bond may already exist between some of your team members.

It's important to revisit team-bonding exercises to keep those bonds strong. And with new teams, it's crucial that bonds are made early on. A strong bond among team members makes it easier for them to trust one another, communicate effectively, and create astounding work. A bond is the foundation of a great team. This chapter focuses on exercises that will strengthen your teammates' relationships with one another, new or old.

IN-HOUSE TRAININGS

94. Talking stick

Purpose: Open communication and learning about teammates

Group Size: 4+

Level: Basic

Materials: A stick (decorate it however you like)

Time: 15 to 20 minutes

Description: The team gets into a circle. Only the person holding the talking stick can speak. The first person asks a question. He or she then passes the stick to the left and the person answers. Once the next person answers, he or she hands the stick to the person on his or her left. This continues until everyone has had a chance to answer. The next person then asks a question and the process is repeated. This process can go beyond the exercise, and the talking stick can be used in all meetings because when a person holds the stick, everyone listens. When they want to say something, they raise their hand and wait for the stick.

Here is a list of potential questions:

- If you could spend 24 hours with any person alive or dead, who would it be and why?

- Who is your favorite storybook character and why?

- What are the two events in your life that were the most significant and life altering?

- What are the three most important things in your life?

- What was the scariest thing that ever happened to you?

- What are your three favorite books and why?

- What are your three favorite foods and why?

- What are your three favorite movies and why?

- If you could have one wish, what would it be?

- If you were a superhero, who would you be?

Discuss your answers and how people felt. How did it feel to use the stick? Did you listen to others when they spoke, or were you thinking about your answer only? Do you think the stick could work in other situations?

95. Purpose mingle

Purpose: Team contribution and communication

Group size: Any

Level: Any

Materials: None

Time: 5 minutes

Description: Before a meeting, tell your employees to walk around the room and talk to one another about what they plan to contribute in the meeting. Have them speak with as many people as possible. You can offer prizes to the person who does so, otherwise use this activity to boost communication and team collaboration before long meetings. This exercise allows team members to think about what they plan to contribute in the meeting instead what they will get or not get out of it.

96. Fortune teller

Purpose: Getting to know personal details about your team

Group Size: 4+

Level: Advanced

Materials: A deck of tarot cards. You can by these at any large bookstore for about $20. Find a deck that has simple pictures.

Time: 20+ minutes

Description: Shuffle the deck well. Hand out five cards to each team member and put the deck in the middle of the team. Have members pick a card that represents how they feel about the team the most. Have them select a second card. This one represents the way they want the team to be in the future. Each member has the chance to return one of his cards to the bottom of the deck and select a replacement from the top of the deck. When everyone has chosen their two cards, convene as a large group again. Have the members share their card selections and explain why they chose the cards they did.

97. Fortune teller alternate version

Purpose: Getting to know personal details about your team

Description: In this version, have the team members choose cards that represent how they see themselves as part of the team now and how they want to be in the future. There are no right or wrong answers in this exercise. It should promote in-depth discussion.

98. What do you value

Purpose: Bonding through company values

Group Size: 6+ (2 or more groups)

Level: Advanced

Materials: Paper, pen, poster board for each group and markers

Time: 30+ minutes

Description: Have each team member write a list of the most important values of the team or organization to which they belong. Have the group narrow this down to the top five values. Have them list these on the poster board and decorate or color the poster to emphasize these values. When they are complete, have the team share its creation with the rest of the groups.

How did it feel to talk about group values? Were your values chosen as one of the top five? If not, how does that feel? Did you tell the group how you felt? Was it hard to pick only five values? Were there common values between the groups?

99. No ifs about it – only buts or ands

Purpose: Communication

Group Size: 4+ (in pairs)

Level: Basic/Advanced

Materials: No extra materials are needed

Time: 10+ minutes

Description: Team members must think of one thing they like and one think they dislike about the team. The partners must state their two statements to one another. The second statement must start with the word "but."

Here is an example:

"I like the humor of the team. But we need longer lunch breaks."

Once each person says the two sentences have him or her repeat them using the word "and."

Here is an example:

"I like the humor of the group, and we need longer lunch breaks."

How did the feeling of the statement change? Did the word "but" feel different than the word "and?" How can this be used in the team's communications?

100. No ifs about it – only buts or ands alternate version

Description: In this version, the words "yes, but" are used. The theme of the conversation is a team retreat. In this exercise each team member makes a suggestion about the retreat. The other team member replies with "yes, but" to begin his sentence.

Here is an example:

"I hope we get to eat Italian;" "yes, but I hope we get a day off;" "yes, but I want to go swimming."

Now the partners exchange the words "yes, but" with the word "and."

For example:

"I hope we get to eat Italian;" "and I hope we get a day off;" "and I want to go swimming."

Did the change in two words change the meaning and feeling of the statements?

101. No ifs about it – only buts or ands alternate version two

Description: In this version, the partners discuss problems in the team. The partner responds with "but you…"

Here is an example:

"The team does not have enough time to get anything done;" "but you work overtime on weekends a lot;" "but you would like to take longer lunch breaks."

Now the partners must change the words to "I."
For example:

"The team does not have enough time to get anything done;" "I work overtime on weekends a lot;" "I would like to take longer lunch breaks."

Ask how the statements made the partners feel? Did "but you" make them defensive? Did using the word "I" give the person more ownership over the issue?

102. Better than that

Purpose: Getting to know your team

Group Size: 4+

Level: Basic

Materials: Nothing extra is needed

Time: 15+ minutes

Description: In this exercise, the leader starts by talking about something he or she enjoys doing. The next person must say that what they like to do is better and state what it is. This continues to go around the team until the leader stops the exercise or someone gets stumped.

Here is an example:

   "I like to eat pizza."
   "I like something better than that. I like to watch old movies."

The purpose is for everyone to learn something new about his or her teammates.

103. There is no 'I' in team

Purpose: Creative thinking

Group Size: 6+ (two teams)

Level: First/Basic

Materials: Two posters and pens

Time: 10+ minutes

Description: One team is given the word "team." The other group is given the word "self." Both teams must create an acronym with the letters in the word. The team with the word "team" must create and acronym that represents qualities a good team needs. The team with the word "self" must create an acronym of qualities that are avoided in a good team. They should write these on the posters, decorate them, and share them with the group.

How did it feel to use the word "self" in a negative way? Did this create an emotional response? Can "self" and "team" exist together?

104. Every which way

Purpose: Learning to express emotion and communicating with one another

Group Size: 4+

Level: Advanced

Materials: Paper and pens

Time: 15+ minutes (10 minutes of prep time)

Description: The leader must come up with at least five scenarios to read to the team. These scenes should elicit emotional responses. They can be real incidents that have occurred with the team.

Each team member must make three rows on their paper: Best, Bad, and Worst.

Then they must think of the best way, a bad way, and the worst way a person could respond to the situation. When the leader is done, the team should share their responses.

Were there similar responses in the different areas? Did people admit to using the bad or worst responses in similar situations? Did this identify any underlying issues people were too afraid to admit before? Did anyone bond because of his or her answers?

COMPANY RETREATS

105. Dart board

Purpose: Dealing with emotions as a team

Group Size: 3+

Level: Advanced

Materials: Dartboard, darts (one for everyone), pens or markers and paper

Time: 10+ minutes

Description: Set up the dartboard in a safe place. Have the team members draw something that makes them angry. They can write the words or draw a picture. When everyone is finished, attach each person's picture on the board. Everyone must throw his or her dart at the picture. Once everyone has done this, the picture is torn and destroyed. The next person's picture is put up next. How did it feel to destroy your picture? How did it fell to have others help you destroy it? How did it feel to share your feelings with the group?

Sometimes it's nice to share what you're feeling with others, especially in a professional environment. This exercise can bring people closer together emotionally, creating a stronger bond among team members.

106. Break it away

Purpose: Deal with emotion

Group Size: 3+

Level: Advanced

Materials: Old bottles, a safe place to break bottles (see below), something to stop up the bottle like a cork, a wad of paper, or cotton and safety goggles

Time: 10+ minutes

Description: You should be extremely careful while doing this activity and wear safety goggles. Have each team member think about something that is making them mad or irritated. Have them yell whatever it is into the empty bottle. When they have finished their rant have them stop up the bottle. Each team member does this until everyone has a bottle. Find a safe place to throw and break the bottles. Don't leave the glass shattered around, though. Recycle it or throw it away.

This exercise allows teammates to let out whatever it is that they are holding in inside. Sometimes stopped up emotions can be distracting and prevent us from doing our best work. Allow each team member to hurl his or her bottle and allow the anger to break away. Most of your employees may be hesitant for this one at first. So as the leader, don't hesitate to step up to the plate and be an example for this activity.

107. Board games

Description: If you're looking for something to just bring the team together that doesn't involve a lot of mind games or physical activity, remember that board games are a great option. Each game has a different purpose and goal and most require some sort of team to be formed. To end a long day of training or a weekend-long retreat, try playing a board game with your team members to blow off some steam and have some fun. A few are listed that would be good for team building.

108. Catchphrase

Description: This is a traditional game that can most likely be found at any local shopping center. Two teams are formed and the goal is that for the teams to guess what their team member is acting out for them based off a disc they pulled. It's basically another version of charades. The teams keep switching back and forth until the timer stops. Whoever has the most points at the end wins.

109. Organizational Jenga

Description: From the When I Work author Rob Wormley, Organizational Jenga is a game to show how important every employee is, at every level, to keep the company moving along successfully. The directions are below:
Using wooden blocks or an actual Jenga game, mark blocks according to the hierarchies present in your company. For example, you might have some blocks denoted as the IT department, and others as HR. You might have particular shaped blocks marked as "manager" and block shapes as "support staff." The labeled blocks should reflect the composition of your office. For example if 10 percent of your staff is IT then 10 percent of the blocks should be, too.

Divide your team into groups and give them an equal number of blocks. From here, either specify the type of structure each team must build or provide guidelines and allow them to build any structure they want. When the time limit has been reached each team, taking turns, must begin to remove a block at a time without destroying their tower.

Do not inform them ahead of time that you will be asking them to do this. If time allows, you may ask them to repeat the exercise. See if they find a way to build a structure that can withstand removal of blocks.

110. Charades

Description: Multiple versions of charades can be found in stores or online. Choose one that you think your team would have the most fun with. Of course there is nothing wrong with traditional charades. It promotes team bonding and different ways of communicating with each other. Whichever game you choose, make sure there's only friendly competition and nothing gets too out of hand.

111. Dinner on a budget

Purpose: Getting to know each other

Group Size: 4+

Level: First/Basic

Materials: An agreed upon amount of money for two teams to buy food and any other kitchen supplies you want for this activity. The company can supply the money or each team member can agree to donate a few dollars for the game. A place to cook and eat that can accommodate two teams.

Time: Two to four hours

Description: The team leader gives each team an agreed upon amount of money. They cannot supplement the money they have received, but they can beg for or borrow food or other items such as seasonings. Give them a set amount of time to gather the food items and create a menu (no more than about an hour). The two teams will then be given a set amount of time to create their menu.

After both teams are finished cooking, they will share the food they made. If you need two kitchens for this activity, have an agreed upon time to bring the team back together to eat. As the team leader, you need to make sure the teams stay on task and stay on time. Also make sure you have plates and eating utensils as well as a place to eat.

If you don't want to make this a competition, food is always a great way to bring people together. If your company can afford to take everyone out to eat or cater in, then take advantage of it and invite all members of your team to get acquainted with one another.

112. Feeling cookies

Purpose: Building trust, open communication and team bonding in a fun manner

Group Size: 6+

Level: Advanced

Materials: Large plain sugar cookies and frosting pens

Time: 10+ minutes

Description: In this activity team members will decorate a cookie that represents their feelings about the team. When they reconvene, have the team members place their cookies on a plate. Team members should then pick a cookie that is not their own. The person who made the cookie will explain the cookie and the feelings behind it. After everyone has a cookie, it's cookie-munching time.

How did it feel to share your feelings (cookie) with someone? Was it hard to trust them with your cookie? Did you have a hard time explaining the cookie?

113. Talent show

Purpose: Getting to know your team

Group Size: 4+

Level: Advanced

Materials: Materials needed depend on each person's talent. Each person is responsible for his or her own props.

Time: 60+ minutes

Description: Each team member should be given five minutes or less and pick a talent that he or she is good at. Team members should try to choose something that the group did not know they had (like blowing big bubbles or hula-hooping) and everyone should applaud. No talent is too big or small. The leader should ask if someone's talent surprised anyone. What was it like to get applause from your peers? How could these talents enhance the team's working relationship and how can they be applied to what the team does?

114. How well do you know your teammate?

Purpose: Team bonding

Group size: 10+

Level: Basic/Advanced

Materials: Paper and pens

Time: 30 minutes

Description: Before this activity, as the leader, you need to come up with a list of 20 questions that your team members may, or may not, know about each other. *A few examples are:*

- What's your partner's favorite color?

- Do they have any pets? If so, what are their names?

- What are your partner's job responsibilities?

You can make them as easy or difficult as you wish. After you have prepared, put your team into pairs. Ask the questions one-by-one and have each partner write down his or her answer on a sheet of paper without asking or telling his or her partner the answer. Give them five minutes to complete each question. Then go around in a circle and have the pairs share their answers out loud. They both have to let each other know if their answers were right or wrong. Repeat this for as many questions as you came up with. When you have asked all the questions, have the partners total up how many they got right. Whichever pair had the most wins a prize. This activity is a fun, team-bonding game that should be played when you have extra time on your hands.

115. Step in, step out

Purpose: Breaking down stereotypes

Group size: 10+

Level: Advanced

Materials: Questions prepared before activity begins

Time: 20 to 30 minutes

Description: This exercise is meant to break down stereotypes among teammates. Before beginning, tell your teammates that this activity only works when everyone is 100 percent honest. And ensure that no judgments are made after the activity is over.

The team leader is going to ask the group a series of questions based on a person's lifestyle and experiences. Each question will require everyone to either take steps forward or backward. The team will start by standing in a straight line with their eyes closed. Eyes will stay closed for the remainder of the activity. Some of these questions may make team members remember details of their lives that they purposefully try to block out. Should anyone get emotional in anyway, give them their space and comfort them when they are ready.

Here are examples of questions, along with how many steps they require, for this activity. More examples of this game can be found online:

1. Take a step forward if you earned a bachelor's degree.

2. Take three steps forward if you earned a master's degree.

3. Take two steps forward if you earned a doctorate.

4. Take a step back if you failed a class in college.

5. Take a step back if you did not earn a college education.

6. Take two steps forward if you had the grades to get into college but your family could not afford it.

7. Take a step forward if you have ever been a victim of verbal, physical, or mental abuse.

8. Take a step back if your family lived off less than $40,000 a year.

9. Take two steps forward if you have ever been victimized because of the color of skin or the religion you practice.

10. Open your eyes.

After your teammates open their eyes, everyone will be spread out in different areas around the room. Ask them to take a look around and then gather together in a circle. Lead a discussion about how stereotyping demises a group's success. Was anyone surprised by where others stood? Were they offended or were they grateful because of where they are today? Take the time to listen to everyone if they have something to say and be sure to encourage and congratulate them at the end. This game is played well with at least 20 questions. Create ones that you know pertain to your group of workers.

PHYSICAL EXERCISES

116. Water sports

Purpose: Teamwork and team cooperation

Group Size: 4+

Level: Basic

Materials: A tray that can hold 10 paper cups, 10 paper cups and water

Time: 20+ minutes (Five to 10 minutes of prep time)

Description: Fill the cups with water just over half full. Place five of the cups in a row. Thirty feet from away, place the other five cups. Place the tray in the middle. This activity may be better outdoors because the water may spill. Have the group gather in the center. Tell them that the objective is to grab all 10 cups and place them on the tray. They must do this by gathering one cup at a time from each side of the room and must alternate sides as each cup is obtained. They must have all 10 cups on the tray and returned to the center. Each team member can use only one foot and one hand at a time. If any water is spilled, they must start over. There are a few different strategies to completing this task, but the team must work together to get it accomplished.

Discuss with the group how they accomplished the task. Was everyone involved? Did they fail a couple of times before figuring out how to do it? Did they start the task without discussing it first as a group? Was everyone involved in the decision-making?

117. Bridge over happy waters

Purpose: Getting to know your team

Group Size: 4+

Level: Basic

Materials: 1-foot long rectangular pieces of paper, markers and tape (optional)

Time: 20+ minutes (10 minutes of prep time)

Description: Give the team the pile of paper and markers. Have them write down something they bring to the team, such as a talent, strength, or skill. If they feel that they have more than two strengths, have them fill out another "plank." When they are finished writing down their strengths, tell them that there is a river rushing through the middle of the room (you may want to mark the river off with tape). Have the members make a bridge over the river that's at least two planks wide. If there are not enough planks, have the team members create more planks by writing down more strengths that they bring to the team. Have the team cross the river over the bridge they created.

Have a discussion with the team about the creation of the planks. Could one person have enough planks to create the bridge? Was it a team effort? How did people feel about writing down their strengths and sharing them with the team? Are there any planks that other team members would add for particular members of the team?

118. One, double, triple

Purpose: Encouraging teamwork

Group Size: 6+ (at least two teams)

Level: Basic

Materials: Pick a team sport such as badminton, soccer, or basketball and an area to play the game

Time: 20+ minutes

Description: The game is played the normal way except that the scoring is different.

For each team member the scoring is as follows:

First score = Six points
Second score = Two points
Third score and beyond = One point each

The goal is to have each team member score at least once because the score will be higher than if one member scores all the time. How did it feel to be included in scoring for the team? Did team members help another member score for the extra points? Did this encourage more teamwork?

119. Helium stick

Purpose: Team building and communication

Group size: 10+

Level: Any

Materials: One large helium stick

Time: 10 to 15 minutes

Description: Have your team get into one straight line. Tell them to hold out their index fingers only. Then you and another management staff member place the helium stick on all of their index fingers facing upwards. The goal is for them to get the stick to the ground without dropping it or using their hands. This can take a couple tries, but it's a great activity to boost communication and team building.

CREATIVE EXERCISES

120. Memory wall

Purpose: Team bonding

Group size: Any

Level: Any

Materials: Sticky notes or a whiteboard

Time: 30+ minutes

Description: Write a few work-related topics on sticky notes or on a whiteboard — i.e. "My first day of work," "Teamwork," "My interview," or "Lunch break." Have your team come together and individually choose a topic they can share a funny or meaningful story about. Go around the room so each person has a chance to share his or her story. You can ask them to draw pictures on their sticky note or whiteboard space or share it out loud with everyone. This exercise is a great one to end the day with as it doesn't involve much thinking or physical activity.

121. Magazine awards

Purpose: Team appreciation

Group Size: 4+

Level: Advanced

Materials: A pile of various magazines, scissors, tape, paper, paper or small poster boards

Time: 20+ minutes (Five minutes of prep time)

Description: Write down everyone's name on a slip of paper and have the team members pick one of the slips. If they choose their own name, they must return it to the pile. Have the team create a trophy out of the magazines for the person they have chosen. It should reflect the best qualities of that person and what strengths he or she brings to the team. No one should know who is making his or her trophy until the trophies are finished. When the group is finished, they should present the awards and explain them to the team.

The team leader should explore people's feelings about receiving the trophy. How did they feel about making the trophy? Did they find it enjoyable to say something nice about a team member?

122. Make a new team

Purpose: Create a team identity

Group Size: 4+ members

Level: Advanced

Materials: A picture of the team (one for each team member), paper, scissors, and glue

Time: 15+ minutes

Description: Each team member is given a picture of the team. They must cut it up into tiny pieces and create a new picture using the pieces. The team should share their creations with each other.

Was it hard to create something new? Was the new picture better than the original?

123. Make a new team alternate version

Description: In this version, the collage is supposed to represent what they hope the team will look like in a few years. Each team member must share and explain his or her creation.

Was this harder to do? What was different between the two pictures? Were team members' pictures similar?

124. What do you think of her?

Purpose: First impressions; getting to know your team

Group Size: 6+

Level: Advanced

Materials: Pictures, pens, and paper

Time: 20+ minutes (20+ minutes of prep time)

Description: The leader should do some research and find 10 different pictures of unknown people. The leader must find professionals from different occupations and know what they do for a living or something that they accomplished that was important.

The leader will give the pictures to the group and the team must write down their impressions of the person and what they think they do for a living. When the team has seen all of the pictures, the team should share their impressions. The leader will then tell the team who the person really is. The person with the most correct guesses wins. You can try this activity in a variety of ways. You can use successful people within the company as examples, or celebrities.

What did people get from first impressions? Is it fair to judge someone on how they look? Did it change the team's opinions when they heard who the people were? Ask people to share the first impressions they had of their teammates and even you.

125. Group story

Purpose: Teamwork; how well do you know your team?

Group Size: 4+

Level: Basic

Materials: Paper and pens

Time: 10+ minutes

Description: The task is for the team to create a story. Each person will say a word, sentence, or a few lines to keep the story going.

The only rules are: stories will begin with "Once" and end with "the end;" each team member has to participate; it has to be related to an incident that has happened, or could happen, at work or with the team; and there will be no prep time. Teams have to make up the story as they go along. The story continues through each team member until the story is ended. It is optional for the leader to write or record the story as it is being told. It can be fun to hear the story in its entirety.

Discuss: Was it hard to jump in unprepared? Did you want to steer the story in a particular direction? Was it frustrating to be given a word that was hard to follow up with or was not the word you wanted the previous person to say?

126. Show me how you Feel

Purpose: Learning to express emotions

Group Size: 6+ (two teams)

Level: Advanced

Materials: Paper and pens

Time: 20+ minutes

Description: Each group is given a list of emotions and a scene they must perform. An example is happy, sad, frustrated, or worried while waiting for the subway. The groups have a few minutes to work out a scene using the list of emotions and the background theme. They must include all of the elements in their play. Everyone should have a role in the scene. After a few minutes, get the groups back together and have each group present their scenes to each other.

The groups must guess what emotions were used. Was it hard for the groups to guess the emotions? Was it hard to act them out?

127. Mood hats

Purpose: Discussions of team feelings

Group Size: 4+

Level: Advanced

Materials: Many different kinds of hats. You can usually find these at a secondhand or thrift store for cheap.

Time: 20+ minutes

Description: Place the hats on a table. Pick a member to choose a hat. They are to state why that hat represents them. Each member will have a turn picking a different hat. After they finish, they should return the hat to the table.

Here is a list of other topics the hats can be used for:

- How do you feel about the team?

- How do you wish to see the team?

- Which hat represents the best part of the team?

- Which hat represents the worst part of the team?

Discuss with the team how they felt about wearing the hats. How did they feel about other teammate's responses? Did the responses influence their hat choices? How does a teammate's choice affect other team members? This exercise can be used with masks also. Or team members can create their own hats or masks depending on your team's age group and access to supplies.

128. Awesome begins with 'A'

Purpose: Team morale booster

Group Size: 5+

Level: Advanced

Materials: Paper and pens

Time: 10 minutes

Description: In this game, the team leader must pick a letter of the alphabet. The team has to come up with words that describe positive things about other team members with the appropriate letter.

For example, if the letter "A" is chosen then the list might look like this:

- John: Awesome

- Kate: All Star

- Sarah: Always on time

- Loreena: Appreciative

You can add as many words to people's names as you wish as long as the word or phrase begins with the letter chosen. For an alternate version, have the team split up into two groups or smaller. Each one will be given a list of names belonging to other people on different teams. Set a timer and have them complete the same task, giving each name as many positive attributes as they can.

How did the team members feel about the words chosen for them? Did they agree with these attributes?

129. Diversity bingo

Purpose: Breaking down stereotypes

Group size: Any

Level: Any

Materials: Pre-printed bingo cards and pens

Time: 30+ minutes

Description: Before you invite your team to play, create a master bingo card with different statements in it that would pertain to members in your group. The statements should be centered on diversity and stereotypes.

Here are a few examples:

- Has a family member in another country

- Is from another country

- Does not celebrate Christmas

- Meditates frequently throughout the day

- Is passionate about a long-term goal

You can make the statements as in-depth as you wish. Once you've finished creating the cards, host the bingo game after your next team meeting. It's played exactly like original bingo, so whoever gets four to five answers right in a row wins the game. Make sure you lead a discussion after the game is played a few times to talk about the importance of diversity and stereotyping, especially if you have a diverse group of employees.

LOW COST WITH PROPS

130. Colors of the rainbow

Purpose: Getting to know your team

Group Size: 4+

Level: Advanced

Materials: Colored candies

Time: 20+ minutes

Description: Team members pick a piece of candy. Tell them to wait and reveal to them that each of these candies has a story. They must tell the story in order to eat the candy. You can give each color a different theme

For example:

- **Red:** most embarrassing moment
- **Blue:** a bad day at work
- **Orange:** your proudest moment
- **Yellow:** a time someone helped you when you were in need

Continue until everyone has eaten the candy. They may pick another piece if they wish. Ask your team members what new information they found about their team members. Was it difficult to share your type of story? Did anyone try to trade his or her candy color?

131. Office trivia

Purpose: Getting to know your teammates, the company, and the department

Group size: Any

Level: Any

Materials: Questions prepared the night before the activity and prizes for winners

Time: 30 minutes

Description: This activity can be fun to introduce new people to their coworkers and to the company. It can also just be a fun way to bring your team together for a half-hour of team building. Prepare multiple trivia questions the night before. The questions can range from company policies, department locations, or questions about team members. Keep the game light but interesting and be sure to keep score. Offer prizes to the winners at the end of the game.

132. Global warming

Purpose: Teamwork and problem solving

Group Size: 6+ (at least two teams)

Level: Basic/Advanced

Materials: Two large bowls (they must be the same size) and water. This is an outdoor activity.

Time: 10+ (overnight prep for the ice)

Description: Freeze water in the bowls. Allow them to become solid overnight. If you like to be creative, add some food color for fun. Take the icecaps and put them in a cooler with a lot of ice to keep them frozen. Each team is given one directive: Melt the ice cap before the other team melts theirs. Each team must figure out a way to melt their ice cap before the other team. Discuss how they solved this task. How did they work as a team? How was the problem process? Was it efficient enough to get the task done quickly?

COMMUNITY SERVICE OPPORTUNITIES

Team building activities are great for building bonds between teammates, but other opportunities are out there that take them out of the office to do so. Community service is a great way to bring your employees closer together because it's also a great way to help those in need. Every community has a plethora of organizations that look for volunteers on a daily, weekly, or monthly basis. Below are a few ideas that are almost always available in communities across the country.

133. Soup kitchens

Description: A soup kitchen is a facility that feeds the homeless or people who can't afford to purchase their own meals. Some are designated for only the homeless and some host nights for people and families in need. For example, if a family is holding a fundraiser for a sick family member, then some facilities host the event for them.

Whatever the cause, soup kitchens are great activities to bring your team members closer together because of the good they will be doing together for others in their community.

134. Road/Park/Beach cleanup

Description: In the past few years, cities across the country have been trying to help the environment. Companies have gone "green," manufacturing companies have started using eco-friendly materials, and recycling has become a more permanent trend.

Local cleanups are prominent all over the country and are easy activities to help contribute to saving the planet. This could be an event that your team helps with and an easy way to bring them closer together. Whether it's a park, road, beach, or historic place in your community that needs cleaning, don't be afraid to encourage your team members to get their hands dirty for a few hours.

135. Makeover a school

Description: In some communities, local schools need help fixing up their campuses. These are great activities to register your team for if you're looking to build, paint, or landscape for a few hours on a weekend. After a couple hours of doing these activities together, your team will most likely feel great for helping out at a local school.

136. Build a house/Habitat for Humanity

Description: Like soup kitchens, building houses for families are also very popular community service activities that need a lot of volunteers. Habitat for Humanity is a popular nonprofit organization that helps build and repair houses. The organization works local, nationally, and even internationally. If you're looking for a community service event and travel time for your team bonding experience, researching this company's projects may be a good idea.

Other organizations also help build and repair houses or living centers that have damaged. If physical team bonding is something your team is interested in, volunteering for a company that builds houses for families in need may be a great event for you to research.

137. Volunteer at an animal shelter

Description: Animal shelters are in just about every community in the country. Animals are brought into these facilities just about every day. According to the American Society for the Prevention of Cruelty to animals, about 7.6 million companion animals are brought into shelters every year — mostly dogs and cats.

These shelters are always seeking volunteers to help with the animals throughout the week or on weekends. It can be feeding, grooming, or even playing with the animals for just a few hours a day.

Animals also relieve stress in people. If your team is under a lot of pressure lately, taking them to volunteer at a local animal shelter may give them the escape they need. Just remember to ask about pet allergies before planning the trip — you wouldn't want any accidents to happen or have a few members count as no-shows.

138. Volunteer at a nursing home

Description: Nursing homes are also looking for volunteers. They mostly ask volunteers to sit and chat with residents inside and visit during holidays. If there is a nursing home or two in your community, look into their volunteer qualifications. This could be a great team-bonding activity for smaller or younger teams.

139. Cook for the needy on holidays

Description: The holidays are a time when volunteer opportunities are endless. Multiple organizations cook meals for the homeless or for families who cannot afford to buy their own holiday meals. If your company has the funds to do so, bring your teams together and cook meals for the needy in your community. If you don't have the space to cook, you could put together meal baskets for these families so they can cook at home.

These types of events bring people together because they feel good after contributing to such a big project. Encourage your employees to donate to the drive or volunteer to pass the food out. All types of help should be encouraged.

140. Donate to children and families in need

Description: This doesn't just have to be a holiday activity, it can be one you decide to host on any day of the year. Set up a clothing drive within your organization or company and encourage employees to bring in apparel for children and adults alike.

To make it interesting, make it a challenge and have employees post on their social media pages. Create a hash tag for the event. They can post pictures of them cleaning out their closets, the large number of bags they are donating, or anything that you think will get employees motivated to participate. You could even make it a competition. Pick whatever you think will promote the best team bonding experience for your employees.

141. Soldier care packages

Description: Our soldiers who are stationed around the world don't usually get to see their families on the holidays. It's nice for large companies to put together multiple care packages for them for the holidays. Multiple websites exist for you to put in your information and learn about the process.

If you don't have the funds or time to put together care packages, you could always have your employees write letters. Any form of communication from anyone is great for our troops to have, and it's nice for them to read a thank-you note on the holidays as they are so far away from home.

142. Organize or participate in a 5K

Description: 5Ks have caught on as fundraisers in the last five years or more. If your company is trying to raise money for a charitable cause, hosting a 5K is a great event to bring your employees closer together. They will be able to plan the event together and think creatively. You can assign everyone a role in the process or give certain teams tasks to do.

If hosting your own 5K is something your company doesn't necessarily need to do, consider registering in a local one. You can register as a team for most races. Encourage all of your employees to participate. Pick one that's on a good weekend for everyone, and if the races have causes, have employees chose the one they'd like to help the most. Most of the time, 5K calendars for communities can be found online — just research it before you make any plans.

AROUND-THE-TOWN MEETING PLACES

To promote team bonding without all of the extra materials, you could keep it old-fashioned. Schedule meet-ups with your teammates at local places around town. Nothing brings people together like drinks, food, and good conversation.

Planning a few of these meet-ups before your team actually gets to work could be a good activity. This way, they get to know each other before the real work actually begins or before you bring them in to participate in team building activities.

143. Coffee

Description: For the most part everyone loves a good cup of joe. And if they don't, most coffee shops have other beverages on the menu like teas and sodas. Coffee shops are usually quiet and peaceful, which makes for a great place to get to know each other and hear one another speak.

144. Happy hour

Description: Going out for drinks is also a great way to break the ice for new teams. Just make sure things don't get out of hand. As the leader, you should be an example and only have a drink or two. If you want, you can have team members bring a plus one to make the event a little more relaxed. Sometimes people feel more comfortable at new events if they have someone they know by their side. Then the next time you plan a happy-hour- get-to-gether, only invite team members.

145. A meal

Description: Food is always a great reason to bring people closer together. Whether it's a new team you've just hired or an old one trying to spend some time together, invite your teammates out to dinner to build a stronger bond.

146. Shopping for an office event

Description: If your office is hosting a celebration of some kind or expecting an important guest, send team members out to purchase all the supplies you'll need. They can bond this way and are more than likely already acquainted with one another.

147. Holiday parties

Description: Any type of celebration is great opportunity to get your team members to mingle, and sometimes it's a great way for them to get to know each other outside of work. If your office has the funds to host a holiday celebration encourage all employees to attend.

148. Monthly birthday celebrations

Description: Similar to above, celebrations are fun for employees to get to know each other or spend time together other than in meetings or in the break room. Birthday celebrations will make every employee feel special and give them something to — hopefully — look forward to that month. Host them monthly if more than two or three people have birthdays in the same month. This way, you'll save a little bit of money and you won't take too much time away from work.

149. Cooking class

Description: If you're looking for something out of the ordinary to build up your team, look into cooking classes. This is a fun opportunity to get your team to work together on something that is not work related. And as mentioned above, what better to bring people together than food?

150. Rock climbing

Description: This is an out-of-the-box idea to get your team up and moving. It will also build a little trust among your team members, which will hopefully build the bond they have together. Rock climbing is a fun, physical activity that most people like to do for fun. It gives their minds a break from the office and allows them to focus on something other than their to-do lists.

YOUNGER EMPLOYEES

151. Circle seat

Purpose: Communication and team bonding

Group Size: 6+

Level: First/Basic

Materials: Space to make a circle

Time: 5 minutes for activity, 10 to 20 minutes for discussion

Description: Have everyone stand shoulder to shoulder, facing toward the center of the circle. Then, have everyone turn so that their right shoulder is inside the circle, their left is outside, and they are facing the back of the person who was to their left. Have the group take a step or two toward the center so that the circle is tighter. Then, on the count of three, everyone sits down on the lap of the person behind them. Lead a conversation about physical contact and why it feels uncomfortable to be close or not, bringing in cultural questions of space between two people.

152. Cinderella, Cinderella

Purpose: Icebreaker, communication and team bonding

Group size: 8+

Level: First/Basic

Materials: Shoes that everyone wore to work that day

Time: 10 minutes

Description: Divide your team into two groups. Have them take off their shoes and dump them in two separate corners. On your count, tell them to run from the opposite of the room toward the pile of shoes. Whichever team can get their shoes on, buckled, and tied and run back to the other side wins. Use this exercise when training or a weekend-long retreat starts to get a little boring, especially if you're working with younger adults.

153. Hot potato

Purpose: Communication and team bonding

Group Size: 4+

Level: Advanced

Materials: A ball or beanbag

Time: 10+ minutes

Description: Have the team sit in a circle. There are a few different ways you can do this activity. As you may know, the object is to throw the ball or bean bag to another person in the circle and have that person say a specified thing and throw it to someone else. For employees, make their responses relate to work. It could be objects found around the office, job responsibilities, or other team members' names — anything that you think your team will have fun doing and build team bonding.

Here's a detailed example:

If the team is in charge of a particular process, like marketing and communication, have them break the process down. Each team member must say what his or her role is and then throws the ball to the next person in the process. You can make this a learning experience, too.

The rules are that if a person drops the potato, the group must start over until they can complete the activity. If a person says the wrong thing, then the group must start over. Discuss how these activities made the group feel. Did they have to pay close attention? Did the other team members feel that another person was not pulling their load and messing the group up? How did they handle it? Were they excluded?

154. Frankenstein's monster

Purpose: Creative teamwork

Group Size: 6+

Level: Basic

Materials: A large piece of butcher paper and a pen

Time: 15+ minutes

Description: The task is to act like Doctor Frankenstein. The team creates a figure with one body part from each member. Each team member must lie on the paper and have one body part traced as part of the team monster. The team can color in and decorate the monster. For more bonding, have the team write in one positive attribute in each other's tracings. It can be something they like about the person or great skills they bring to the team.

What was the end result? How did it feel to be a part of a larger entity? How did your body part fit on the creature? Who decided what body part people were going to use? Was there a vision of what the creature looked like before they started? What positive things to others have to say about their peers?

155. Badminton by the numbers

Purpose: Physical teamwork and communication

Group Size: 6+

Level: Basic

Materials: Badminton set and a die

Time: 30+ minutes (20 minutes of prep time)

Description: The game of badminton is played under normal rules except that before a team serves the bird, the leader roles a dice. The rolled number is the amount of times the team has to hit the bird before they serve it over the net or the other team gets the point.

This exercise specifically builds teamwork and communication for team members. It's a great activity for young teams just starting out. They can burn off energy and communicate while being active. Discuss how hard this was to do. Was it harder than regular badminton? Did it take extra teamwork and communication to accomplish? Did it utilize more team members than a normal game would? How did everyone feel about being included in the game?

156. One, two, untie your shoe

Purpose: Teamwork

Group Size: 4+

Level: First/Basic

Materials: Everyone with shoes

Time: Five to 10 minutes

Description: This will not work with women wearing skirts or dresses. The group is broken up into teams. Everyone lies down with his or her feet in the air. The first team to untie everyone's shoes in the group without the use of hands wins. Feet cannot touch the ground during this game.

157. Younger employee meet-ups: lunch, beach, or bowling

Description: Younger employees are usually more willing to participate in physical, outdoor activities like picnics, beach trips, or bowling. Every community has something a little different to offer, and you'll know the perfect spot for your team as you get to know them more. These kinds of activities will build your team's bonds with one another and potentially make them build relationships with one another that aren't solely based around work.

Chapter 6
Communication Is the Key: Listening and Talking Exercises for Your Team

If you've heard it once, you've probably heard it a thousand times, but communication is key in any working relationship. Effective communication is a major factor in what determines if a team is successful. If team members cannot openly speak to one another about ideas, conflicts, or have a conversation in general, then they probably will not be a team that works together well.

Without communication, many team members will feel lost and alone. It has to begin from the top and continue strong all the way down the ladder of directors, supervisors, and workers.

The following activities are designed to help your team communicate with each other more effectively. Remember communication is not always verbal. Sometimes people communicate with body language, gestures, or even a light touch. These activities incorporate all types of communication styles for your teams to practice.

IN-HOUSE TRAININGS

158. Do you hear what I hear?

Purpose: Listening skills and identifying distractions

Group Size: 2+

Level: Basic

Materials: Pens and paper

Time: 20+ minutes

Description: Have the team members write down noises they hear in the room. Give them a couple of minutes. Visit each area in which they work. Have them continue to write down sounds they hear. When you have completed the rounds, have the team members compare their lists.

Were team members aware of many sounds? Are some of them distracting? Can some of them be silenced? How can these sounds distract team members from their work?

159. The right questions

Purpose: Communication and getting to know each other

Group Size: 4+ (in pairs)

Level: Basic

Materials: No additional materials are needed

Time: 20+ minutes

Description: The leader will explain the difference between open and closed questions. Open questions allow the person to explain their answer. Here is an example: What types of food do you like? A closed question usually requires a one-word answer like "yes" or "no." Here is an example: Do you like Italian food? One person in the pair is given a scenario. *For example:*

The person is going on a vacation to Disney World. He is bringing his family, and they are staying for three days. They are going to visit the Magic Kingdom, Epcot, and Hollywood Studios. The other partner will be given two minutes to figure out what the scenario is. They can only use closed-ended questions. Both of the partners try to figure out scenarios using only closed-ended questions. After both partners have a chance to ask a question, the leader will give them new scenarios. This time they can only use open-ended questions. Again, they will be given two minutes to figure out the scenario.

Which types of questions were easier to use? Were you able to discover the scenario quicker by using open-ended questions? Would a mix of the two have made it easier?

160. Can you follow directions?

Purpose: Listening skills

Group Size: 4+ (two groups)

Level: Basic

Materials: Paper and pens

Time: 10+ minutes

Description: Write down 10 different sets of instructions on separate pieces of paper. Make the directions no more than three steps long. Give each team five sets of directions. Have the team read the directions one at a time to the other team. They must only say the directions once. Once they read the directions, the other team has to do what the directions said. Then it is their turn to read directions to the other team. Do this until all 10 directions have been read. The group with the most successful demonstration of the directions wins.

Here are some sample sets of instructions:

- Get up. Turn around. Shake the person's hand to your left.

- Hop on one foot twice. Then lock elbows with your teammates. Turn clock wise as a group.

- Nod your head twice. Laugh once. Nod your head eight times.

Was it hard to hear the directions only once? Did you get the directions right but out of order? Did the entire team agree on what they heard before the team executed the directions?

161. What is my crazy line?

Purpose: Communication and creative thinking

Group Size: 4+ (in pairs)

Level: Basic

Materials: Sentences prepared ahead of time

Time: 20+ minutes (10 minutes of prep time)

Description: The leader must develop some wacky sentences. These sentences are written on pieces of paper. Have pairs face one another. One of the pair is given a sentence, and then they must have a natural conversation that includes the sentence somewhere. They are given a two-minute time limit. This is repeated with the other pairs. The pair that successfully does the task more times wins.

Was it difficult to control a conversation in order to use the sentence? Did you want to give up? Did you have to pick a certain subject to talk about?

162. Active listening

Purpose: Listening skills and conflict resolution

Group size: Any

Level: Any

Materials: A prepared speech

Time: 30+ minutes (Or however long your team meetings usually are)

Description: Before your next team meeting, prepare a speech filled with company jargon and boring statistics and facts. Every couple of sentences, read something that's completely off the subject of your meeting topic. What you ate for breakfast, what color your socks are, or what you are doing later that night are all good examples.

After you finish, hand out a piece of paper and quiz your employees on the speech you just gave. The purpose is to see if anyone noticed your random statements throughout the speech. Afterwards, lead a discussion about the importance of active listening, especially during team meetings. Be sure to mention that a lot of conflicts arise because of miscommunication and lack of attention. Use this activity as an example as you discuss how to improve active listening during meetings and avoid conflicts in the future.

163. Interpretation

Purpose: Accepting different interpretations; communication and listening

Group size: Any

Level: Any

Materials: Pens and paper

Time: 15 minutes

Description: Have different phrases prepared before your group arrives. These phrases should be ones that can have multiple meanings.

Here are a few examples:

- "I'll get back to you in a bit."

- "This material is outdated."

- "Back to the drawing board."

You can also include phrases that are trending at that point in time that your employees may or may not know. Write them on a whiteboard or have them projected onto a flat screen so they are easy to see. Once your team arrives, ask them to read each phrase and write down what they think it means. Give everyone about 15 minutes to complete the task then go around the room and have everyone share their answers.

This exercise is a great discussion-starter about accepting others' interpretations of different things, as well as a good conversation starter about open communication and active listening.

164. Times are changing

Purpose: Learning to deal with change

Group Size: 6+ (partner exercise)

Level: Advanced

Materials: Paper and pens

Time: 20+ minutes

Description: In this exercise, the team members must create timelines of their lives. They must have at least four life-changing events listed. Then the team members pair up. They will discuss one life event with one another.

They must answer the following questions:

- Was it hard to change?

- What made it significant?

- What helped them through the change?

- Looking back, was the change for good?

Each team member will have a turn with his or her partner's timeline. Was it difficult to talk about change? Was it difficult to share personal information? Did the teammates feel empathy from their partner?

165. What swims

Purpose: Listening skills

Group Size: 3+

Level: Basic

Materials: No extra materials are needed

Time: 15+ minutes

Description: This game is similar to Simon Says. The leader says a list of animals that swim like "fish swim, dolphins swim, people swim, anteaters swim." During the calling of the animals everyone is doing a swimming motion. When the leader reaches an animal that does not usually swim, such as an anteater, everyone must stop swimming. Whoever continues is out until there is one person left. The leader can choose to use other verbs such as crawl, jump, and hop instead of swim. The leader can also use other team members to call out names.

166. Tell me about it

Purpose: Listening skills

Group Size: 4+ (in pairs)

Level: Basic

Materials: Paper and pens

Time: 20+ minutes (15+ minutes of prep time)

Description: The leader will create simple lists of topics to talk about.

Here is a sample list:

- What I ate last night

- What is my favorite movie and why

- Where I went to school

- What is my favorite book and why

Give the list to the pairs. One of the members in the pair will talk first. He will talk for five minutes while the other person listens. When he is finished, the person listening must summarize what she heard in a minute. The roles are then changed. The only rule is that when you are listening you cannot talk.

Was it hard to remember what the person said? Was it difficult not to say anything?

167. Tell me about it alternate version

Description: In this version, the person listening is blindfolded. They must listen carefully.

Was it easier to listen when you could not see anything? Was it harder? Did you notice that the less things that distracted you, the more you were able to truly listen?

168. Tell me about your day

Purpose: Getting to know your team and listening skills

Group Size: 4+ (in pairs)

Level: Advanced

Materials: No extra materials are needed

Time: 15+ minutes

Description: The team members are paired off, and one is chosen as the talker and the other as the listener.

The talker tells the other person in eight minutes what he or she does in a typical day at his or her job. The listener must actively listen. He or she must only say things that encourage the person to talk more. After the time is up they switch roles.

Was it hard to talk about your job for that length of time? Was it helpful to hear other people talking about their job? Did you learn anything new? Did you feel you were being heard?

169. Move me

Purpose: Communication and employee motivation

Group Size: 4+

Level: Advanced

Materials: Paper and pens

Time: 20+ minutes

Description: On paper, have the team write what kind of motivation they prefer. They should list at least 10 different kinds.

The leader should then discuss the two main types of motivation, the kind we get from other people and the kind we find within ourselves. Have the team go over their lists and decide what kinds of motivation they have listed. Have the team members add the two types together and report to the group which kind they prefer.

Did people learn from one another? Were people surprised by their own answers? Were people surprised by other people's answers?

170. Team blackjack

Purpose: Nonverbal communication

Group Size: 9+ (in three or more teams)

Level: Advanced

Materials: No materials needed

Time: 10+ minutes

Description: Break the team into at least three small groups. Like in the game blackjack, the goal is for the team to reach 21 using their fingers. They cannot communicate verbally with one another to accomplish this task.

Have each group get into a circle facing one another and hold their hands behind their backs. The leader will say, "Ready, set, go."

When the leader says, "go," the members are to hold out their hands in the middle of their circle. They are to hold zero to 10 fingers each. The team that has 21 on their fingers first wins. This may take a few turns before a group is able to do this. This is similar to the evens/odds game. This forces teams to communicate without their voices. It's interesting to watch how they all individually choose to communicate.

Discuss with the group how they felt not being able to talk during the exercise. What kind of nonverbal communication did they use? How can a team accomplish a task without communicating clearly with each other?

COMPANY RETREATS

171. Drought

Purpose: Teamwork

Group Size: 4+ (if there are too many people you may need more than one group)

Level: Basic/Advanced

Materials: Two cans, water, chalk, four giant rubber bands (these can be found at a craft store or you can use any long elastic object). This is an outdoor exercise that needs to be played on level concrete.

Time: 15+ minutes

Description: The leader draws a large circle with the chalk. One of the cans is filled halfway with water and placed in the middle of the circle. The task is for the team to get the can out of the circle and pour the water into the other can outside the circle. They cannot touch the cans with their hands, they cannot enter the circle at any time, and they must use the rubber bands.

Discuss how the group accomplished the goal. How did it feel to have limited resources? How did the group communicate during this exercise? Did anyone lose their temper or become frustrated?

172. Play with clay

Purpose: Team building and communication

Group size: 8+

Level: Any

Materials: Clay

Time: 15+ minutes

Description: Divide your team in groups of five to six people per group. Give them each a large lump of clay. When everyone is settled, call out an object that they have to make out of the clay. Only one person can work at a time on the clay masterpiece. Call time every 30 to 40 seconds so group members rotate. After everyone has had a chance to work on the clay, judge each team's sculpture to see who completed it the best.

This activity will bring a lot of commotion, but it will teach group members how to communicate effectively from afar and work together on a deadline.

173. Group sculpting

Purpose: Teamwork

Group Size: 4+

Level: First/Basic

Materials: Clay for each team and a whistle

Time: 10 to 20 minutes

Description: Each team is given a lump of clay. The leader will tell the groups an object or a theme that needs to be sculpted. When the whistle is blown the first person in the team begins to sculpt quickly. After 20 seconds the leader blows the whistle and the next person takes the clay and continues sculpting the object. This continues until every team member has had a turn.

174. Life-size Pictionary

Purpose: Communication and listening skills

Group size: 6+

Level: Basic/Advanced

Materials: Whiteboard, markers, word cards, and a creative imagination

Time: 25+ minutes

Description: Make two teams. Write down random words on all of the cards. Pick one player from the opposite team and tell them they have to draw what is on his or her card on the whiteboard. He or she has to make his or her team members guess the word with the drawing. Team members drawing on the board are not allowed to turn around, talk, or give hand gestures. Only drawing.

This is a good activity to promote some friendly competition among your team members and teach them effective communication skills.

175. Stickies

Purpose: Listening skills

Group Size: 6+

Level: First/Basic

Materials: Sticky notes and a card or board game of your choice

Time: 20+ minutes

Description: This is a game within a game. Team members are given three sticky notes to put on their clothes. Whenever a person talks out of turn, is not listening, or is saying something inappropriate, the person who noticed they were not listening takes a sticky from them. This will continue throughout the board game. The person with the most sticky notes in the end wins.

Discuss how it felt to give feedback to others. Did you notice you were talking out of turn?

176. How does that make you feel?

Purpose: Learning to express emotion

Group Size: 4+

Level: Advanced

Materials: A recording of different sounds, pen and paper

Time: 10+ minutes (20 minutes of prep time if a recording needs to be made)

Description: The leader plays various sounds, and team members write down how the sound makes them feel. The team will share the results and any reasons they felt a certain way.

Was it hard to hear some of the sounds? Did they bring back memories? Did you have an emotional response?

177. Listen and build

Purpose: Communication

Group Size: 6+ (two teams)

Level: Basic

Materials: Clay for each group

Time: 15+ minutes

Description: The members of the two teams face their backs to one another. The first team creates a sculpture out of the clay. They must then describe it to the other team so that they can recreate the same sculpture on their side. This is repeated for the other side. Then the teams can look and see how they did.

Was it hard to describe things to others? Did people interpret what they heard differently?

178. Listen and build alternate version

Description: In this version a painting is created. This task is harder because a painting is harder to correct. The teams must communicate clearly and listen before they attempt to recreate the painting.

Was it harder with paint or clay? Did everyone participate and help guide the painter? Did everyone have a different vision?

179. Listen and build alternate version two

Description: In this version the leader creates a sculpture out of colored clay. The leader then gives each team the same colored clay and describes the sculpture for both teams at the same time. The final sculptures are compared.

Observe if the groups took different approaches, and discuss them afterwards. Did the groups make the same sculpture as you or were they different?

180. White water rafting

Purpose: Communication

Group Size: 4+

Level: Advanced

Materials: Blindfolds, obstacles (rocks), and cookies

Time: 10+ minutes (10+ minutes of prep time)

Description: Set up a river with obstacles that the river raft must avoid or it will crash. The team is blindfolded and the river guides set themselves near the rocks. The guides must navigate the boat by verbal commands around the rocks. If the team gets past the rocks, they deliver a cookie (passenger) to the river guide. They then make their way to the next guide.

Each guide can only give directions when the boat is in his or her part of the river. If the boat crashes, the team does not get the cookie and the boat continues to the next guide. The guides can give words of encouragement when the boat is in another part of the river, just not directions. And yes, the team can eat the cookies when they are finished (even the guides who crashed the boat). Switch the members to be different guides and riverboats.

Discuss how it felt to be a boat and how it felt to be a river guide. How did it feel to watch another river guide direct the boat and not be able to help? How did it feel to get the cookie (reinforcement)? How did it feel to see the boat crash and not get a cookie?

181. A storm is coming

Purpose: Teamwork and creative communication

Group Size: 6+

Level: Advanced

Materials: Old newspapers and masking tape

Time: 50+ minutes

Description: The team is told that a hurricane is coming. They must build a shelter using paper and tape to cover everyone before it hits. They have 25 minutes to plan and 25 minutes to build the shelter. No one can speak while they are building.

Was the team able to build it? What was the strategy? How did the team communicate while building? Was preplanning important?

PHYSICAL EXERCISES

182. People Tic-Tac-Toe

Purpose: Friendly competition and a test of company knowledge

Group Size: Teams of five to eight members

Level: First/Basic

Materials: A dry erase board or blackboard. Draw a large tic-tac-toe board. Create about 30 questions. Here are suggestions:

- Information about individual team members

- Information about the company or organization

- Information about what was supposed to be learned about team building

- Information about the jobs people have

Time: 10 to 20 minutes

Description: The group is broken up into two teams. Each team designates a speaker. The teams take turns trying to win tic-tac-toe by calling out a particular square. The leader asks a question — if the team gets it right, they get the square. If the team gets it wrong, the other team has a chance to get the square by answering it correctly. The team that gets a tic-tac-toe wins. Play multiple rounds so a friendly competition is stirred between the two teams. For more of a challenge, ask questions that are work related.

183. Egg Toss

Purpose: Teamwork and creativity

Group Size: 4+ (at least two teams are formed in this activity)

Level: Basic

Materials: One raw egg for each team and materials to build the egg carrier such as:

- Cotton

- Egg cartons

- Bubble wrap

- Feathers

- Tape

Time: 20+ minutes

Description: Each group is given an egg and may use any of the materials to build a carrier. They are given a certain amount of time to accomplish their task. The goal is to create a carrier that can be dropped with an egg inside without breaking the egg.

After teams create the carriers, it is test-flight time. Have each team drop their carrier from at least 8 feet high. The team's egg that does not break will win. Have the group discuss how they made the carrier and how they worked as a group. How did it feel to win or lose? Was there a consensus in the group about how the carrier should be built?

184. Team body art

Purpose: Teamwork and creativity

Group Size: 4+

Level: Basic

Materials: No extra items are needed

Time: 10+ minutes

Description: The team is challenged to become a certain work of art by using only their bodies. Everyone in the group must be a part of the work of art. The leader may set time limits for the team to create the artwork.

How did it feel to be a part of the team in this exercise? Was it hard to include everyone? Did everyone have a part in deciding how to create the artwork?\

Here is a list of possible art pieces:

- Octopus
- A car
- A windmill
- A truck
- A spider
- A waterwheel
- An orchestra
- A clock
- A football field
- A rock concert
- Christmas Day
- Halloween party

185. Team body art alternate version

Description: The game is played the same as the first except that the team is broken into two or more groups. The first team is given an object, but the other teams do not know what it is. They have a certain amount of time to make a work of art, and the other teams must guess what it is. Teams are awarded points for correct guesses. The team that had the most art pieces identified correctly wins. This may confuse the team members if they think that the guesses were more important than the creations.

How was it different to have another team guess what the object or scene was? Was it harder to do? Did the team change around to make it easier for the other team to guess or did they work against the other team to win the game?

186. Ships and sailors

Purpose: Team building and active exercise

Group size: 10+

Level: First/Basic

Materials: None

Time: 20 minutes

Description: This game is similar to Simon Says, also. It's fun to play at company retreats or with a younger group of employees. There are many ways to play, so multiple sets of instructions can be found on the internet.

To start, have all of your team members spread out in front of you. As you read off commands, they have to follow.

Here are a few command examples with descriptions:

- **Captain's coming:** Players stand saluting the captain (you or whomever is directing the game). They cannot move until "at ease" is said. If they do they are out.

- **Ships:** Run to the left.

- **Sailors:** Run to the right.

- **Hit the deck:** Players all drop to the ground.

- **Stand watch:** Players break up into pairs. One will jump on the other's back and they will "stand watch."

- **Three men eating:** Players get into groups of three and pretend to eat.

- **Four men rowing:** Players get into a straight line of four and pretend to row a boat.

- **Five men pointing north:** Players get into groups of five and point upward to the sky.

As you can see, some commands require players to get into groups. This is how people are eliminated from the game until there are only one or two people left in the game. Observe how your team groups themselves together when you call commands out. It's interesting to see who gets left out and who does not. Lead a discussion afterwards about it if you have time.

187. Cat's cradle

Purpose: Teamwork, communication and listening skills

Group Size: 4+

Level: Basic

Materials: A large rope and blindfolds for everyone on the team

Time: 10+ minutes

Description: The team is blindfolded and the rope is tied end-to-end and placed at the team's feet. The challenge is to get the team to make a triangle with the rope. When the team thinks they are done, have them look at what they did. You can try a square, octagon or any other shape.

Discuss with them how it felt to work together to accomplish the task. Did it turn out the way they thought it would?

188. Team geometry

Purpose: Teamwork

Group Size: 5+

Level: Advanced

Materials: 50- to100-feet of rope

Time: 15+ minutes

Description: All team members must grab a part of the rope. No one may switch places with anyone else. The team must form the shape of the number eight with the rope and with no rope left over. You can decide if your team can speak during this exercise or if they are not allowed to speak verbally, or you can try both.

How did the team figure this task out? Did everyone have to cooperate? Did everyone communicate?

CREATIVE EXERCISES

189. Writing for the future

Purpose: Getting to know each other

Group Size: 3+

Level: First/Basic

Materials: Pens and paper

Time: 20 minutes (this can be done ahead of time and members can bring their reports to the meeting)

Description: Members are asked to think about where they will be in 10 years, focusing on the following: job, residence, appearance, and family. Have team members bring their reports to the team building meeting and discuss the projections and what it felt like to think in those terms. The leader should give the team time to respond to each person's report.

190. Writing for the future alternate version

Description: Members can bring a picture they have either drawn or a photo they have altered by using a pen or manipulating it in a photo program to show what they might look like in 10 years. The leader of the group can collect pictures of the team members and put them on display. This helps the members laugh, relax, and take feedback in a positive manner.

191. Group portrait

Purpose: Group creativity

Group Size: 4+ (if a larger number of people participates, you may want to consider teams)

Level: Basic

Materials: Various colors of marker, pen, pencil or paint, and a large piece of paper or butcher paper

Time: 15 to 20 minutes

Description: Pick an order of the group. The first person makes a mark or line on the paper, and then it is the next person's turn. The rule is that no one's line or mark can intersect or cross another person's. The goal is to get the group to make a picture together. They should not talk during this exercise. When everyone has had a turn or two, have them name the picture to describe what it is. Afterward, have them talk about the process. Discuss how it felt to be put in a certain order. Discuss how they came up with a title.

192. Back-to-back drawing

Purpose: Creative teamwork

Group size: 8+

Level: Any

Materials: Paper, pens, colored pencils, markers, etc.

Time: 10 minutes

Description: Put your group into pairs. Have them sit back to back with their own piece of paper and coloring materials. They each will take turns and describe something for the other to draw. They are not allowed to tell their partner what it is that they are drawing; they can only give vivid descriptions and details. Have them include colors, shapes, and lines to make it more of a challenge.

Each partner gets five minutes to draw or explain the object, and then they switch. After each has had a turn have them show each other their drawings. Whichever pair's drawings were closest to the original object wins. To keep track of the descriptions, you can write out objects or people on slips of paper and have your group members choose them from a hat. This way, you'll actually know who was the closest in their drawings.

193. The complete story

Purpose: Listening skills

Group Size: 6+ (two or more groups)

Level: Basic

Materials: Paper and pens

Time: 20+ minutes

Description: In this exercise, the groups must come up with a story. Each person is assigned a scene in the story and should draw the scene individually. The groups come together and show their stories. If the group listened, they will understand their roles in the story.

194. The complete story alternate version

Description: In this version, the leader reads a story. Each person is assigned a number. The leader says the number before they read a passage from the story. The person whose number is called is assigned to draw that scene. When the story is completed, the team members must then draw their scenes. They come back together to see if they drew the scenes correctly.

195. Mad-lib mission statement

Purpose: Company knowledge and team bonding

Group size: 4+

Level: Any

Materials: Company mission statement and a worksheet

Time: 20 to 30 minutes

Description: Take your company's mission statement and turn it into a Mad-Lib game. To do this, remove key nouns, verbs, and adjectives from the statement and then create a worksheet where the removed words are shown as a blank line with instructions on what kind of word is needed.

You can split your team into groups of two or keep everyone together as a whole to do this activity. If you pair them off, have one team member ask for a word to fill in the blank and have the other supply it. Have them take turns. If you decide to keep everyone in one large group, have each person take turns supplying words.

Once there are enough words read the mission statement back. It will sound silly, but it will get your group members to recognize the meaning behind your company's mission, goals, values, or objectives. You can have multiple rounds of this game.

The purpose of this exercise is to strip away jargon and confusing words from the mission statement so your group members can fully understand the meaning behind the company's mission. It will make them more comfortable with their responsibilities at work and, if they're new, make them feel more welcomed.

196. Paper talk

Purpose: Communication

Group Size: 3+

Level: Basic

Materials: A piece of paper for each team member

Time: 10+ minutes

Description: First, give the following instructions to the team: Pick up the paper and hold it in front of you. Close your eyes. Now fold your sheet of paper in half. Tear off the upper right-hand corner. Fold the paper in half again. This time, tear off the upper left-hand corner. You will now fold the paper in half again. Then tear off the lower right-hand corner of the sheet. Open your eyes.

Do not answer questions that the group may have during the exercise. As they do the exercise, you do not do the exercise with them. No one will have the same paper. Discuss the importance of two-way communication.

Was it fair not to be able to ask questions? Was it hard to rely on only verbal instructions? Would a demonstration of the activity help?

197. Follow the beat

Purpose: Listening skills

Group Size: 3+

Level: Basic

Materials: A drum, but it's not necessary

Time: 5+ minutes

Description: This exercise is simple. The leader starts off by striking a simple beat. The group repeats that beat by hitting it on their table or leg. The leader then does another beat, and the team must repeat the pattern. The leader can make the beat more and more complicated. Everyone should have a turn leading the team.

Here is an example: Hit you right thigh with your right hand, then your left thigh with your left hand, then clap twice.

Was it hard to repeat what was heard? Did you follow your neighbor's lead? Did you want the pattern repeated?

198. Zip, zap, zop

Purpose: Communication

Group Size: 4+

Level: Basic

Materials: No materials needed

Time: 15+ minutes

Description: Everyone in the group stands in a circle. One person is chosen to start the game and points to someone else in the circle and says, "Zip." The second person points to a third person and says, "Zap." The third person points to a fourth person and says "Zop." And then it starts over again with "Zip."

The goal is to get this going around the circle as fast as possible. If a person gets zipped, zapped, or zopped and does not immediately pass it on they are out. Keep going until there is one person left.

199. Chinese whispers

Purpose: Communication

Group size: 6+

Level: First/Basic

Materials: None

Time: 10 minutes (depends on the size of your group)

Description: Have your team sit in a large circle. Pick one person to start; he or she will think of a long sentence and whisper it into the person's ear who is sitting to their right. Then that person whispers what he or she heard to the next person. They can only say it once — no repeats. This continues until the last person has heard the sentence, then they will share it aloud with the rest of the group. Most likely, it won't be the same sentence that the first person made up. This game is fun to try and identify where the sentence changed.

Stress the importance of communication in the workplace in a discussion after you have played a few rounds. Ask your team for examples where a problem or conflict occurred at work because of miscommunication. Provide tips to avoid miscommunication in the future.

LOW COST WITH PROPS

200. Show me your signs

Purpose: First impressions

Group size: 4+

Level: Advanced

Materials: Materials needed depend on the exercises chosen, sticky labels

Time: 20+ minutes (in addition to the activity chosen)

Description: The leader picks another activity from the communication or team building section in this book. The leader creates labels and sticks them on the back of each team member without that person knowing what it says; only the other team members can see the sign. The team members should interact with other members according to their signs. When they complete the other activity that was chosen, ask each team member what they think his or her sign says. Then allow the team members to look at their own labels.

Discuss with the team members how they felt to have a particular sign. Did they feel they were treated differently? Did they treat others differently according to their sign? How do these signs affect the team in their interactions with one another?

201. Definitions

Purpose: Getting to know your team

Group Size: 4+

Level: Advanced

Materials: Index cards and pens

Time: 20+ minutes

Description: Each team member is given five cards. They must write what they think an effective leader is. Each card will contain a different aspect of what makes a good leader.

The team leader will collect and shuffle all of the cards. He or she will add his or her own set of cards to the stack. The leader will then deal out three cards to each team member. They must rank the cards according what they believe are important aspects of a good leader.

The leader will then place the remaining cards on a table and the team members may select cards to trade. They must have three cards when they are finished trading. No one can talk during this stage of the exercise. The object is to have three cards that are the closest to what they believe makes a good leader. The leader should give them a time limit. Have the team members share their cards and state why they feel that these three represent what they believe a good leader is.

How did they feel about the card they were left with? Did teammates agree with each other about what aspects make a good leader?

202. Definitions alternate version

Description: In this version, the team will define what makes an effective team. The team will choose as they did before. When they have all of their cards, the leader will take them away and allow the team members to pick two cards from what is left. Each team member must state why these cards are important. The people who wrote the card must identify themselves and explain what they wrote.

How did it feel to have your choices taken away? Were the choices that were left good ideas? Why or why not? Why would others list these cards along with the ones they created?

203. Scream for ice cream

Purpose: Teamwork, team initiative, and nonverbal communication

Group Size: 4+

Level: Advanced

Materials: Ice cream maker, rock salt, ingredients to make homemade ice cream, a recipe card, bowls, spoons, and ice

Time: 30+ minutes

Description: Place all the items around the room and put one empty bowl and spoon in front of you. This is a good exercise to do at the end of the day or after lunch. Say nothing except, "Go." Look at the bowl and at your watch and say nothing further. The goal is to see if the team has enough initiative to make ice cream without being told. They have been given the tools and the permission.

If they do not understand at first, you can give them subtle hints. Look into the bowl and then at your watch. Lick your lips a couple of times. Rub your stomach, but do not say anything.

After they make the ice cream, ask them some questions. Who decided to initiate a move and start making the ice cream? Who ran the project? Was everyone involved? How long did it take them to figure out the task? Were they scared to make a move without instructions? What finally sent the message about what the task was? Do they always need to be told what to do, or do they have group initiative and leadership?

Chapter 7
Trust Your Teammates: Trust Exercises That Will Motivate Your Employees

"Team building activities are designed to help a group of people trust and communicate more effectively, in order to facilitate a more productive work or organizational environment."
– Stephen Coenen

As Stephen quoted above, team building activities help build trust among team members. Without trust, group members will be explosive; conflicts will be a norm, arguments will break out frequently, and the quality of work will be poor. It's important for team leaders to encourage their groups to trust one another openly. Nothing is better than working with a group of people you that you know will support you through every decision and idea you throw on the table, as well as have your back should things go south.

Team building exercises that are designed to build trust are typically more emotional than other exercises. Make sure you thoroughly explain each exercise before jumping into it in this section. And ensure your teams that no judgment or negative comments will be made when they are practiced. Take a stand for your team members should any negative behavior happen. And as the leader, make sure you set the tone for each exercise and participate actively with your team members.

IN-HOUSE EXERCISES

204. Global vote

Purpose: Talking openly about feelings and opinions

Group size: Any

Level: Advanced

Materials: None

Time: 20+ minutes

Description: (The following activity was created by Jim Lyness of the EDS Account Leadership Program. The description is from higherperformanceteams.org.)

Create two flip charts that are positioned 30 to 50 feet apart. Then the number one and the words "Almost Never" are written on one flip chart. On the other, write the number seven and the words "Almost Always" are written.

Ask your group members to imagine a scale between one and seven and think about the statement: "We tell each other the truth." A statement will be said by you, or the other person leading this activity, and group members will have to vote with their feet, meaning they will get up and physically position themselves on the scale.

After the question or statement has been asked, the facilitator asks each group member to declare where they stand on the scale (ones, twos, etc.) pertaining to this question. Then the facilitator chooses someone, looks him or her in the eye and asks, "Why are you standing there?" After hearing the answer, the facilitator moves on to the next person and asks the same question. All of your group members should be given the opportunity to answer the question on telling each other the truth.

Then the facilitator makes the statement: "We respect one another," and instructs the team to vote with their feet again on a different question. Again, depending on time constraints and the size of the team, everyone might be given the opportunity to answer the question: "Why are you standing there?"

The statements and voting continue with: "We seek to understand one another;" "We support one another;" and "We are trustworthy." Notice if any of your group members change a lot on the scale depending on these statements.

Give the team a short break if you have multiple questions you would like to ask for this activity, but make sure you don't explain the purpose of this activity until after you have finished asking all of your questions. The value of this exercise is that team members can understand each other's attitudes, beliefs, and convictions on these questions and statements. It's very important for team-relationship dimensions. This will guide individual team members in determining the best way to deal with one another when these dimensions come into play later as the team continues to form and progress.

205. Never have I ever

Purpose: Building trust

Group size: 4+

Level: Any

Materials: None

Time: 10 minutes

Description: Get your team to sit in a circle and ask them to hold up five fingers. Take turns going around the circle saying one thing that has not happened to them while at work or in their professional careers. The person who is left with the most fingers at the end of the game wins, and the person who loses all five fingers first loses.

Here are some examples:

Never have I Ever...

• Been one hour late to work

• Received a raise

• Moved states because of a job

• Broke office equipment

The goal of this exercise is for team members to open up to one another and form a level of trust. Make sure to mention to keep the game appropriate while at work.

206. Patience

Purpose: Practicing patience and trust

Group size: Eight team members per group

Level: Any

Materials: One large piece of paper, eight markers, and string

Time: 20+ minutes

Description: First, divide your group up into teams of eight. Each one of them will hold onto an end of a string. On the other end is a marker that all eight individual strings are tied to. Below them is a piece a paper. Your team has a certain amount of time to write out the word patience. If they work together, and practice patience, they can write the word under the allotted time you have set. For more of challenge in the second round, have the groups draw a picture.

After the activity, lead a discussion about the importance of patience at work. Ask your teams what the most challenging parts of this activity were and how they overcame them.

207. Eye contact

Purpose: Eye contact and trust

Group size: 6+

Level: Advanced

Materials: None

Time: Five to 10 minutes

Description: This is a simple activity but an effective one. Have your team get into pairs and stand facing each other. For 60 seconds they have to stare into each other's eyes without breaking eye contact, laughing, giggling, or looking away. There may be some interruptions in the first few rounds, but by the third, most people should get the hang of it. To challenge them even more, tell them to have a conversation for 60 seconds without breaking eye contact.

Some people are no good at keeping eye contact or even making it at all. And eye contact is a sign of trust. This activity will help those who are bad at it get into the habit of doing it all the time. It may be difficult for them at first, so as the leader it's important for you to be patient with all of your team members and understand how each of them might react to this activity. Lead a discussion after about it and ask your team to be open with how they felt when they first started the activity compared to when they finished it.

208. Company concentration debate

Purpose: Building trust and open communication

Group Size: 6+

Level: First/Basic

Materials: Playing cards with visuals that match

Description: First, find a deck of playing that has visuals instead of numbers. (You can find them online or create them yourself.) Lay them out in a formation on a flat surface face down. Split your team up into two groups — smaller groups will work, too, if you have a large team. Just make sure your have more than one deck of playing cards if you do so.

Each member will take a turn flipping over the card. They are to remember where certain cards are so when they flip one over they can find its match. Once a match is found, then that person is to discuss and debate why the two cards are associated. If the majority of the other team agrees with his or her reasoning, then they get a point, but if not they can debate for a few minutes.

This exercise is not only a concentration game to improve memory and thinking, but also a game to build trust and open communication among team members. It's good to practice how to have calm debates without emotions and words being taken out of hand.

209. Blind leading the blind

Purpose: Getting to know each other, team building, and trust building

Group Size: 8+ (must have an even number)

Level: First/Basic

Materials: Blindfolds

Time: 10 minutes

Description: Team members are paired up. One person puts on a blindfold. The other person will help them to the other side of the room. The rule is that they can only give voice commands. The helpers cannot touch the other person or use any other cues. They spin the person around a couple of times and then tell them where to go. They can help them navigate doors and stairs, but be careful. After the helpers have directed their blindfolded team members to their destination, the partners switch.

210. The blind line

Purpose: Communication and problem solving

Group Size: 4+

Level: Basic

Materials: Blindfolds for everyone

Time: 10+ minutes

Description: Blindfold the team members and have them stand in a line. Have them rearrange themselves according to what parameters you give them.

Here is a list of parameters that you could choose from:

- Shortest to tallest

- Oldest to youngest

- Longest with the company to the newest

- The team member with the largest family to the smallest family

Discuss how they solved getting in the line you described? Did someone take charge to get the others in line? Did team members feel vulnerable not being able to see?

211. Trust Fall

Purpose: Building trust

Group size: 2+

Level: Basic/Advanced

Materials: None

Time: Five minutes

Description: Most people probably played this exercise as a young child, but it's worth a revisit. Pair your team up so everyone has a partner and instruct each pair to take turns falling backwards into each other's arms. This exercise builds trust between two people really fast.

To build trust among all group members, switch up the partners after each of them has had a turn falling. This way bonds are formed between everyone in the group and not just between two people.

212. Tip me over

Purpose: Trust and support

Group Size: 6+ (at least two groups)

Level: Advanced

Materials: No extra materials are required

Time: 10+ minutes

Description: Break the team into two groups. The groups should form two parallel lines that are facing one another. They need to be close enough to touch their hands with the group in front of them. Have everyone hold up his or her right hand. Have each member touch hands, palm against palm, with the person standing in front of him. Do not lock fingers.

Now have the team members hold up their left hands. Have them touch palms with the person on the left of the person in front of them. There will be people on the end of the rows that will only be using one hand. Now have everyone take a step back. They should be leaning forward to be supported by the people in front of them. If you want to challenge them further, have them step back again. Their legs should be straight, no bent knees are allowed. Have them step forward again before releasing hands or people might fall forward.

Discuss with the group how it felt to rely on others. Did they trust others to hold them up and support them? How did the people on the ends feel about only using one hand? If you would like, you could switch people around so different people are on the ends.

213. Task master

Purpose: Communication

Group Size: 6+

Level: Advanced

Materials: No extra materials are needed

Time: 20+ minutes

Description: The first person chooses another team member and gives them a number of tasks to complete. For instance, they may say, "I want to do five tasks." The person chosen must then choose five tasks for that person to perform such as, "Pick up a piece of paper, write your name on the paper, fold the paper five times, turn around three times, and unfold the paper with your eyes closed."

These directions are only given once. The person must complete the tasks as given. This is a listening exercise. The winner is whoever completes the most number of tasks. The game continues until everyone has had a chance to give and perform tasks.

214. Task master alternate version

Description: In this version, the players do not only their tasks but also everyone else's tasks before them. If anyone messes up, the game begins again. This improves listening skills when other people are talking.

COMPANY RETREATS

215. Blind man's build

Purpose: Communication

Group Size: 4+ (at least two teams)

Level: Basic

Materials: Blocks and blindfolds

Time: 15+ minutes (five minutes of prep)

Description: The team is broken up into two groups, the sighted and the blind. The sighted group builds a simple structure using the blocks. The blind team looks and tries to memorize it. Then the blind team is blindfolded.

The sighted team takes the blocks and places them around the room. The blindfolded must then find the pieces and rebuild the structure. The sighted team tells them where to go to get the pieces. They cannot touch the player or the block at any time. If it is taking a long time to complete, the leader may put a time limit on it. Once the team members find the pieces, the sighted members try to tell them how to build the structure. Switch the teams and repeat the activity.

Discuss with the team members how they completed the activity. How did they tell each member to find the pieces? Did they do them one by one? Did everyone participate?

216. Blind obstacle course

Purpose: Trust and communication

Group size: 8+

Level: Advanced

Materials: Blindfolds and random objects to make an obstacle course

Time: 30+ minutes

Description: Split your group up into two or three groups depending on the size of your team and the size of the room you will be doing this activity in.

Each team member will take turns completing the obstacle course blindfolded. Their teammate behind them can guide them with their voices and give them tips to complete the course safely.

They will have a few seconds to analyze the course before they put on the blindfold — if anyone falls or misses and obstacle then they have to start all over. Make sure you set the course up safely. Don't include obstacles that are too difficult to do while blindfolded or objects that could hurt someone.

Observe each team's method of communication and who was more willing than others to trust his or her teammates. Discuss after what it was like going through an obstacle course blindfolded and what it meant to have a team behind you helping you get through it safely. Apply this train of thought to situations that could happen at work and talk about how to avoid them by using what they learned in this activity.

217. Blind wine waiter

Purpose: Teamwork, communication, and leadership

Group size: 6+

Level: Advanced

Materials: Per team — One bottle of wine, one corkscrew, one wine glass, and five blindfolds

Time: 30 minutes

Description: Divide your team into groups of six and ask them to pick a leader. Then hand out five blindfolds to each person on the team who is not the leader. The leader will sit a few feet away from his or her team on his or her hands. Then instruct your teams to find a bottle of wine, corkscrew, and wine glass so they can pour their leader a glass wine.

All of these items will be hidden around the room for them to find. Make sure they are hidden in places where nothing can break or no one can get hurt. The leader can guide his or her team to the items with his or her voice but has to remain sitting.

Only one team member can complete one task.

The tasks and rules are as follows:

- **Task 1:** Find a bottle of wine and bring it to the team leader
- **Task 2:** Find a glass and bring it to them team leader

- **Task 3:** Find a corkscrew and bring it to the team leader (this person will also cork the bottle after it is opened)

- **Task 4:** Open the bottle of wine

- **Task 5:** Pour the bottle of wine and give it to the team leader

- **Task 6:** The team leader has to drink the glass of wine without using his or her hands

Whichever team completes all the tasks correctly then they win the game. You can award prizes if your feel it's appropriate. Observe how each team completed the exercise. Did anyone stand out to you? Did anyone's strategy work better than others? Did the leader use effective communication and leadership skills to guide his or her team? Or did someone else take the lead during the exercise?

218. Money auction

Purpose: Learning to express emotions

Group Size: 4+

Level: Advanced

Materials: A $5 bill

Time: 15+ minutes

Description: This is an auction for the $5. Start the bidding at $1. The leader should get the group worked up over the auction and make it exciting. In the end, the bidding will go beyond $5 (you can give the money if you wish, although the leader is the winner).

Why did people bid more money than $5? Did emotions cloud people's reason? Is this technique used in the market place? Do people get worked up over things that are really smaller than they make them out to be?

219. Who's got a dollar?

Purpose: Forming trust

Group size: 5+

Level: Any

Materials: $1 bill

Time: 10+ minutes

Description: Ask your group, "Who's got a dollar?" It may take a few moments, but someone will offer you one. Go over to that person and ask them what his or her hopes and aspirations are for this team. Once they've given answer, take the dollar walk over to the next person and ask them the same question. Only repeat this one or two more times. Then ask someone for a $10 bill and continue to ask group members the same question about their hopes for the team. Repeat the exercise one more time with a $20 bill.

After everyone has answered the question, return the money to its owners. Lead a discussion about taking risks in the workplace and trusting one another. Explain how important these facets are to the team's success and growth as a whole.

PHYSICAL EXERCISES

220. Night trail

Purpose: Trust, support, leadership and communication skills

Group size: 8+

Level: Advanced

Materials: Blindfolds, ropes, poles and course obstacles

Time: 50+ minutes

Description: Split your team into two groups. Each group will be blindfolded and have a rope connecting them. They are to navigate their way through an obstacle course, created by the team leader, blindfolded. The first team to complete the obstacle course wins.

Clarify that this exercise is not based on speed but on each person's commitment to his or her team. Watch for people who take charge and navigate and support his or her team through the course safely. Lead a discussion about these people's leadership skills and about anyone else who stood out to you during the exercise.

221. Running Free

Purpose: Trust building

Group size: Any

Level: Any

Materials: Blindfolds

Time: 20 minutes

Description: Let your team get into teams of two. Once they've done so, each team needs to pick one person to be the leader and the other to be a follower. The follower will be blindfolded for this entire exercise and the leader will be guiding him or her throughout it.

Instruct the leaders to hold their partner's hand and go on a slow walk for three minutes. This allows the followers to get a feel for the area and get used to someone else being their eyes. After the first three minutes, tell the teams to go on a normal-paced walk for another three minutes. After that round, tell the leaders to progress to a fast walk for 30 seconds and then to a 30 second jog. After each one, the blindfolded partner is forced to trust his or her partner more and more. After the jog, instruct the partners to go on a 15 second run and then a very fast 15-second run — with breaks in between of course.

After the fast run, the followers can take off their blindfolds and give them to their partners. Repeat the whole exercise with the partners switched. Lead a discussion after everyone has had a turn about trusting others in difficult situations and how that could happen at work.

222. Slice 'n' dice

Purpose: Trust building

Group size: 10 to 20

Level: Any

Materials: None

Time: 20 minutes

Description: Ask your team to get into two equal lines and put their arms straight out in front of them. Their arms should overlap with the person's standing next to them. One-by-one, team members will walk through the intersected arms. Team members with their arms out will have to adjust themselves accordingly when each person walks through. Once they have gone through they will join the end of the line again.

This process continues until everyone has had a turn; then it's repeated. This time, however, team members should walk quickly, run, or sprint down through the line trusting that people will let them pass safely. This exercise let's your team members have fun while also building up their willingness to trust others.

223. The many legged monster

Purpose: Teamwork and cooperation

Group Size: 6+ (this activity needs at least two teams)

Level: Basic

Materials: Two taped lines that are parallel and 15 feet from one another

Time: 15 minutes

Description: The group must go from one line to another as a group. They have touch points on their bodies. A touch point is anything that touches the group. This can be any body part like a leg, arm, or elbow. Once a touch point is used, it cannot be reused and is only counted once. Pick a number of touch points that a group can use to get from one line to another. You can count the number of people and subtract two to three touch points that they can use. For example:

Five people in a group may be allowed to use three touch points. The groups must work together and be creative. The fewer the number of touch points allowed, the harder it will be.

Discuss with the groups how they completed the activity. Was communication important? Were skills and flexibility of individuals considered? Did the group feel uncomfortable being close and possibly having to touch other team members?

224. Willow in the wind

Purpose: Trust building

Group size: 10+

Level: Advanced

Materials: None

Time: 15 minutes

Description: This exercise works best with people who know each other fairly well. Select one person to be the willow in the first round. He or she will stand in the middle of the circle, which is made up of the rest of the group members. The person in the middle will perform multiple "trust leans" on his or her coworkers. It's the coworkers' job to support the willow and then pass him or her around without any trouble. Have your team members take turn being the willow if they would like. This exercise allows your employees to build trusting relationships with each other while having fun.

225. Till death do us part

Purpose: To build trust and teamwork

Group Size: 4+ separated into pairs

Level: Basic

Materials: Something to tie people's hands together

Time: 10+ minutes

Description: Have people tie one of their hands to the hand of a partner. The fun begins as you pick different tasks for the partners to accomplish. Here is a list of suggestions:

- Jump rope

- Put a shirt on over their clothes

- Tie their shoes

- Make a meal

226. Till death do us part alternate version

Description: Tie all the members of the team together. Everyone will have both hands tied to someone else. Have the team try to do activities as one large unit. Here are some suggestions:

• Create a piece of art

• Get everyone through a door

• Have everyone write his or her name on a poster

• Make a pitcher of tea and pour a cup for everyone

The activities are endless. The point is for everyone to work as a unit to accomplish a task together.

CREATIVE EXERCISES

227. You drive, I'll shift

Purpose: Teamwork

Group Size: 4+ (in pairs)

Level: Basic

Materials: Pen and paper

Time: 10+ minutes

Description: The team leader picks a simple shape to draw like a line or circle. One partner holds the pen steady on the paper. They cannot move the pen. The other team member must move the paper underneath the pen to draw the shape. The one that comes the closest to drawing the shape wins. You can alternate partners.

Were simple shapes hard to draw? Was it frustrating to stand still while someone else completed the job? Did you try to tell them what to do? Did they get angry?

228. Blind man's tag

Purpose: Communication

Group Size: 4+ (divided into pairs)

Level: Advanced

Materials: Blindfolds and an open area to play

Time: 10 to 20 minutes

Description: One person in each pair will be blindfolded. Explain to the team that they need to play in a certain area. You can mark this off with chairs or other articles if you wish. Choose one of the pairs as the pair to be "it." They are the ones that will try to tag the other blindfolded people. The sighted people in the pairs try to get their blindfolded partners away from the "it" person. The sighted "it" partner tries to direct his partner to tag the others. If they are tagged, they become the "it" person. The sighted partners can only use voice commands to tell their blindfolded partners where to go. Halfway into the game have the partners switch positions. Afterward, talk about how it felt to be the sighted one and then being blindfolded. Use it as a tool to discuss communication and trust issues among the team members.

LOW COST WITH PROPS

229. Protect your assets

Purpose: Team rapport and team building

Group Size: 8+

Level: Basic

Materials: Sticky notes

Time: 10 to 15 minutes

Description: Pair off people on the team. One will choose to carry the "asset" first. That person gets a sticky note on their back. The object is to try to get the other team's sticky notes while protecting your sticky note (asset). The team left with their sticky intact wins. You can then switch the partner who is carrying the asset. Have a discussion about how people felt to be protected by a team member and also how they felt protecting someone else.

230. The three monkeys

Purpose: Communication

Group Size: 6+

Level: Advanced

Materials: Blindfold and simple office objects such as pens, paper clips, or staplers

Time: 20+ minutes

Description: The objects are set on one side of the room. Two team members are chosen to help. Team member one is blindfolded and placed near the objects. Team member two is placed in the center of the room. And the rest of the team is at the far end of the room.

Here are the rules:

Team member one can talk but cannot see. Team member two can see and talk but can only look at the team members on the far side of the room. The remaining team members can see but not speak. Team member two must direct team member one, according to what the other team members convey. The team leader gives a task that team member one must accomplish but only shows it to the mute team members. The game is completed when team member one finishes the task. Different team members may try other roles with new tasks.

How did it feel to be team member one? How about team member two? How did it feel to be in the mute crowd? Was it a team effort to accomplish the task? What strategies were used?

YOUNGER EMPLOYEES

231. Mini-marshmallow pass

Purpose: Communication

Group Size: 6+ (in pairs)

Level: Basic

Materials: Mini-marshmallows, spoons and blindfolds

Time: 10+ minutes

Description: The task is for the partners to pass 10 mini-marshmallows to the other person to eat. The problem is that both partners are blindfolded. They must scoop up the marshmallow on the spoon and feed it to their partner. When one partner has completed eating 10 marshmallows, the partners change roles.

Was it difficult to do without the use of sight? What techniques did the partners figure out to accomplish the task? How did it feel to rely on the other person? Was it scary to be fed while blindfolded?

232. Chocolate gold rush

Purpose: Teamwork

Group Size: 6+ (in pairs)

Level: Basic

Materials: Wrapped chocolates. If someone on the team cannot eat chocolate, make sure you include treats that they can eat. You also need a carpet scrap big enough for two people to stand on but not much larger. If no carpet is available, the leader can tape off a small area.

Time: 20+ minutes

Description: The carpet is put in the center of the room. The goodies are placed all around the scrap just far enough that it would be difficult for one person to reach. The team is broken up into pairs.

The rules are as follows:

- No body part may touch outside the carpet at anytime or you lose your turn

- No object may be used to pull the chocolate toward the pair

- The chocolate must be picked up, not slid or dragged

- There is a time limit

The way to do this task is for one of the pair to hold the other while he or she grabs the chocolate. This should not be told until after the exercise. You may need to add candy, as some pairs will be better than others.

How did they figure out the activity? How did it feel to rely on someone to hold you up to achieve a goal?

233. Tap me next

Purpose: Team morale booster

Group Size: 6+

Level: Advanced

Materials: None

Time: 20+ minutes (10 + minutes of prep time)

Description: The leader creates a list of positive affirmations that team members can identify with.

Here is a sample list:

- A person who makes me smile

- A person who makes me laugh

- A person I trust

- A person I admire

- A person who is a hard worker

The leader asks one person to stand up. The rest of the team lies down their heads. The leader reads one of the affirmations. The person standing picks a person who fits this description. The chosen person stands and joins the first person. The leader reads another one and those standing pick one person each who fits that description until everyone is eventually standing. A new person is chosen to start and the game can be repeated using new affirmations.

How did it feel to be chosen for a particular affirmation? Did you have any difficulty finding someone who fit a particular affirmation?

234. Who's missing?

Purpose: Getting to know your team

Group size: 10+

Level: Basic

Materials: None

Time: 10 minutes

Description: Instruct your team to get into a circle facing inward and close their eyes. Walk around the circle and lightly tap one person to get up and leave the circle. Suggest to them to do this as quietly as they can. After one person has left, ask the group to guess who left the circle with their eyes still closed. Keep repeating this exercise until there is only one person left. This is a great activity for younger employees and newly formed teams.

Chapter 8
Problem Solving: Challenges for Your Team Members to Solve Their Own Problems

Issues are bound to happen at work — especially among coworkers or on tight deadlines. It's important for team leaders to remind their teams that problems are going to happen and that they can be resolved. However, it's also important for team leaders to encourage their team members to attempt to come up with solutions on their own before approaching them frantically. This next chapter is dedicated to problem solving and includes activities that will help teams of all sizes and levels figure out how to solve problems quickly and smoothly, together, before going to the boss.

Of course, encourage your teams to come to you — or other members of upper management — if and when an issue is out of their hands or could jeopardize the company, the team or the team's latest project. Be sure to follow up with your team when problems arise to keep track of the situation, and of course, use your best judgment if you are a team leader or boss when problems arise.

Follow up is the most important step in any team building exercise. We must follow up and measure the impact of a team building to understand its effectiveness.

Some examples:

- **Solving a problem:** How we can actively involve everyone to solve the problem by letting them define what they can and cannot do (have controls so that necessary steps are not missed), making them part of the solution and system.

- Set goals that are agreed on by the team for a defined period of time, and see if the goals are being met or not.

- Root cause analysis: Once you set the goals, do a root cause to determine the success and failure, which results in lessons learned, and implement them for the next round (making it an iterative process).

> I always recommend team building as part of the culture of an organization. It is a continuous process rather than an event. Team building exercises are critical to launch a new product, formation of a new team for an initiative, problem solving, and new hires, reenergizing an existing team...
> — *Pramod Goel*

IN-HOUSE TRAINING

235. It's your problem

Purpose: Problem solving and communication

Group size: 10+

Level: Basic/Advanced

Materials: Paper and pens

Time: 20 to 30 minutes

Description: Split your team into smaller groups and give them a common problem that could happen at work. Tell them they have about 20 minutes to come up with a problem-solving challenge for the problem that the entire team can participate in. The challenge has to involve teamwork, creativity, and communication. When the 20-minute time limit is up, have each group present its challenge. Together, choose the best one and do the activity together. This exercise puts leadership and responsibility back on your team members, which is good practice for them to learn how to solve minor issues on their own rather than always coming to you, or another management employee, for solutions.

236. What's wrong with the picture?

Purpose: Visual skills

Group Size: 4+

Level: Basic

Materials: No extra materials are needed

Time: 10+ minutes

Description: Have the team look at you very closely. Then leave the room and change something on your clothing. When you return, have the team decide what is changed. Have them come up with a group answer. Do this a few times; each time make it harder for them to spot.

Did it take a lot of concentration? Were some people better at the task than others?

237. What are you doing this week?

Purpose: Creative time management

Group Size: 4+

Level: Advanced

Materials: Three blank weekly schedules for each team member

Time: 30+ minutes

Description: Hand out the three blank schedules to each team member. In the first one they will fill in a typical week at work.

When everyone is finished, the second week is a week they have complete control over. This is a vacation week in which they are doing things they want to do. This can be anything. There are no monetary or time constraints. Talk about these two lists with the group. How are these weeks similar and how are they the different?

The third week is a combination of these two weeks. In the middle of things, they have to do they need to insert things they want to do. These should be reasonable activities. Challenge the team to use this new schedule in the upcoming week.

Was it hard to create the third week? Are you more likely to do things that actually worked in your schedule than to just talk about them?

238. Were you paying attention?

Purpose: Observation skills

Group Size: 6+ (two or more groups)

Level: Advanced

Materials: Flip chart and simple objects around the room such as balls, pens, paper, etc.

Time: 20+ minutes

Description: During another exercise or when the team enters the room, have a set of instructions on a flip chart. It should be no more than five steps. Do not say anything about the instructions; just have them in a visible location. Begin the exercise by taking away the instructions. Break the team up into groups. Tell the groups that they have one task, and that is to complete the instructions that you just removed. Team members will have to rely on memory and communication to complete the task. Give the team five minutes to complete it. The team that most closely completes the task wins.

Ask them: Were you paying attention? Did people have different recollections of the instructions? Was there a consensus?

239. Shop or else

Purpose: Communication and teamwork

Group Size: 4+

Level: Advanced

Materials: A computer with internet access or a catalog

Time: 30+ minutes

Description: Tell the team the following story:

"You have been chosen to go to an underground bunker. It is hundreds of feet below the earth's surface. You will have enough food and water for a year. At the end of the year, you will be able to go back to the surface of the earth. During the year, you will only have two sets of clothes. You have $250 to spend on anything else you will need for the year. You will only be able to bring what you buy. You have to use the money to buy supplies for everyone on the team. You cannot go over budget."

Give the team the catalog or allow them to access a store's website such as Wal-Mart, Sears, or Target.

Discuss how it felt to shop for the group rather than meeting their own needs. How was the decision made to buy the items? Was everyone given an allotment to spend for himself or herself? Did they have to vote on what was bought?

240. Shark-infested waters

Purpose: This exercise emphasizes teamwork and problem solving between team members.

Group Size: 8+ (if it is a larger group, break it into groups of eight to 10)

Level: First/Basic

Materials: Small raft-shaped pieces of cardboard about a foot in diameter, construction paper, fake sharks, two 2-liter bottles of water or soda, islands, and tape You can make water out of construction paper or place fake sharks on the floor. You need a large area to move through. Mark off the two islands with tape.

Time: 20 minutes (10 minutes of prep time)

Description: Give the team enough rafts for every team member minus one. *Read them the following story:*

"You have been stranded on an island. Across the water is another island that contains the drinks you need. You have miniature life rafts that float but cannot move in the water. If you slide them, they will sink into the ocean. In the water, there are bloodthirsty sharks. On the island, there are man-eating bunnies. The bunnies will not hurt a group of people such as yourselves, so you need to make it to the other island as a group. Once you get your drinks you must bring them back to the first island."

Have them start on one island and place the boats in the water and move them as needed so the entire group can get to the other island, retrieve the drinks, and return to their island. This promotes group thinking and teamwork.

COMPANY RETREATS

241. Keep it real

Purpose: Creative problem solving

Group size: 8+

Level: Advanced

Materials: Pens, paper or laptops

Time: 45 minutes

Description: This activity is simple, yet it allows your team members to branch out of their comfort zones and get a little creative. Split your team up into small groups. They are to choose a prominent problem that's happening in your community, company, or state and create a strategic plan to solve the problem. If you want to assign each group a common problem then do so. After the 45 minutes is up, invite each group to share their strategic plan with the rest of the groups. Encourage positive feedback from all team members.

242. It's a mystery

Purpose: Problem solving and teamwork

Group size: 10+

Level: Any

Materials: Clues (made by you)

Time: 45 to 60 minutes

Description: This activity is similar to the game Clue; however, the team leader will make up the case. Get as creative as you would like, but make the case relate to a situation that could happen at work. Create clues for each team to find. To incorporate work-related material into the game, the clues can be facts and statistics about your company or directions to another department in the building. Split your team into smaller groups and give each the first clue and about an hour to solve the mystery. Whichever team solves the mystery first wins a prize of your choosing.

243. Hot topic

Purpose: Communication

Group Size: 4+

Level: Advanced

Materials: Paper and pens

Time: 20 to 30 minutes (10 minutes of prep time)

Description: The leader should do some preparation and choose a topic that is current, applies to the team, and may be controversial. The leader explains that the team is going to deal with the issue in a new way. Have the team members make a statement about the issue in a positive way instead of a negative way. Try to keep it simple and non-offensive.

For example:

"People are taking extra time at lunch." This can be rephrased as: "Being on time to work helps keep people on task and efficient."

Have the group scale their feelings about the "hot topic." The scale can be from one to 10. One would be very little feeling about it and 10 would be very upset. Have them write the number on a slip of paper and fold it. Have them put the slips of paper in a container. The leader mixes up the papers. This helps keep the team members anonymous. The leader then calculates the average score. The leader should keep this number to themselves at this point.

Ask the team members to predict what they think the average score is about the subject. Announce the average score and reward the team member that came the closest to the average number.

Break the team into three groups: ones, 10s, and judges. The ones and 10s should spend about five to 10 minutes coming up with an argument in support of their side. The ones are not in support of changing the situation. The 10s are in support of creating some sort of change. Each team will have five minutes to argue their case to the judges.

The judges write down the two sets of arguments. They review the two arguments and make a decision about the winner.

Note: This can go beyond a team building game and be used as an actual team decision tool.

244. Hot topic alternate version

Description: In this version, you can make it like a courtroom drama. You can add props and make it very dramatic. Do not let it get too silly, or the impact of the exercise could be lost.

245. Buy it part one

Purpose: Communication

Group Size: 6+ (at least two teams)

Level: Advanced

Materials: A chalkboard or flipchart, pen or chalk to write on board, objects to be used for building, play money (each group gets $100 in alternate version), paper and a pen for each team

Time: The first part will take 20+ minutes (10 to 15 minutes of prep time)
Description: This is part one of two exercises. They can be used together or as individual exercises.

Break the team into two smaller groups. On the board or flipchart, write down the objects that need to be bought. The object of the exercise is to get the group from one side of a specified area to the other. The area should be at least 12 yards wide. The group must buy the materials in order to build the bridge that will get them across the space. They cannot touch the ground with their feet at any time. Flip a coin to see which team goes first. Each team must bid on the objects presented. They can only spend their $100 on the objects.

For example:

Team A
$10 on rope
$40 on board
$50 on paper

Team B
$75 on paper
$25 on rope

The bidding is blind. Each team must write down their bids and turn them into the leader. The leader then distributes the objects to the teams based on their bids.

Discuss with them if they think they can build the bridge based on what they bought. How did they work out the bids in their groups? What was their bridge design? Did they draw it out? If they did not have enough materials, how did they continue to build their design?

246. Buy it part two

Purpose: Communication, cooperation and creativity

Group Size: 6+ (at least two teams)

Level: Advanced

Materials: Objects to be used for building, pen and paper for each team

Time: 20+ minutes (10+ minutes of prep time)

Description: If the group did part one, then they already have their objects to build a bridge. If they do not have the objects, then you can give each team the same objects to use.

The object of the exercise is for each group to build a bridge over an area that is at least 12 yards wide. The team must be able to cross it without touching the floor at anytime. Give them a time limit to accomplish the task. A successful

team (or teams) can build the bridge and demonstrate how it works.
Discuss how they felt about building the bridge. Did they draw it first? Did everyone participate? How did they feel about the process? Did they get competitive? How did that feel?

247. Pinky's up

Purpose: Learning to deal with change

Group Size: 4+ (at least two groups)

Level: Advanced

Materials: 10 to 15 piece children's puzzles, a watch

Time: 20+ minutes

Description: The groups are each given a puzzle. In this exercise, the teams are asked to complete their puzzles. Once they have done this have, them do it again and ask them to improve their time. Now tell them on the third run no one can use their pinky fingers. If anyone's pinky finger touches a puzzle piece, the group must start over. Whichever team finishes first wins.

Was it hard to complete the same task when there was a change? Were some team members able to change easier than others?

248. It is puzzling

Purpose: Problem solving and communication

Group Size: 6+ (at least two groups)

Level: Advanced

Materials: A bag and two to three children's puzzles. They should not contain more than 25 pieces each.

Time: 30+ minutes

Description: The team leader mixes the pieces of the different puzzles. The team does not know this. He then gives each group a bag of pieces. The task is simple — they must complete their puzzle (you may decide to give them a time limit).

The groups will figure out that they have the wrong pieces. If they ask, repeat that they need to complete the task.

Did the groups figure out what to do? Did they do it on their own? Did any puzzle get completed? Were team members afraid of taking initiative?

PHYSICAL EXERCISES

249. Invisible ball

Purpose: Facilitates cooperation between team members

Group Size: 3+

Level: First/Basic

Materials: No materials needed

Time: Five to 10 minutes

Description: The person who is picked to start decides on the type of ball that she holds in her hands. The rest of the group should be able to see or imagine the ball, too. The person should define the size and weight of the ball with her movements not by using words, as this is a silent exercise. Is it a baseball? A golf ball? A beach ball? Once the person with the ball has defined the shape, weight, and any other important characteristics through movement, she passes or throws the ball to another person in the circle who then catches the ball. The second person changes it to another ball and then passes it to a third person. This keeps going until everyone has had a chance to create and throw a ball.

250. Raft Flip

Purpose: Teamwork and physical problem solving

Group Size: 4+ (if you have enough people you can have two teams)

Level: Basic

Materials: Tarp or sheet 5-by-5 feet or larger

Time: 10 to 15 minutes

Description: Stand a group of people together on a tarp or sheet. Have the team figure out how to flip the raft without anyone falling into the water (touching the floor). This is a good one if you have two teams, because you can time each other for some healthy competition. The trick is to start with a corner and fold it over the rest of it with one person moving it as people in turn pick up their feet and shift a little.

251. Move the hoop

Purpose: Teamwork and problem solving

Group Size: 6+

Level: Basic

Materials: A hula-hoop

Time: 10+ minutes

Description: The team stands in a line and holds hands. The leader places the hoop on the first person's arm. The task is to get the hula-hoop down the line and back again without letting go of each other's hands. You can split the team and have a competition to see who can do it faster. Was it hard to do? Did some people struggle to get it moving? Did the team encourage them?

252. Over, under, and through the woods

Purpose: Team abilities

Group Size: 4+

Level: Basic

Materials: Two ropes and two poles or trees at least 10 feet from one another

Time: 15+ minutes (five minutes of prep time)

Description: The leader must tie the two ropes parallel to one another between the poles or trees. The top rope must be high enough to make it a struggle to get over but so that at least one team member will be tall enough to make it over without touching the ropes. The two ropes must be far enough apart so one team member can slip between them and the bottom rope should be high enough for someone to squeeze under without touching.

The task is for the group to get to grandmother's house on the other side of the electric fence. At least one team member must go over, one must go under, and one must go through the ropes. The other team members may duplicate any of these. If one person touches the rope and is "shocked," the team must start over until everyone can get to grandmother's house safely.

How did people's individual skills play into this exercise? Was the team able to complete the task? How many tries did it take? Did people have to try different ways until they could get through the fence? Was this frustrating for other people in the group? Did someone have to change the way they went because someone else could not make it?

253. The 20-foot monster purpose

Purpose: Trust and cooperation

Group Size: 5+ (the larger the group the more fun the activity)

Level: Basic

Materials: Strips of cloth and a room to move around in

Time: 10+ minutes

Description: Have the team stand in a straight line. Tie each team member's legs together with the person next to him or her. Tie the two end people together. Now have them walk as a group across the room. This can be challenging for some groups. If you need to, you can break the large group into smaller groups. Make sure there are no obstacles or anything someone could fall on and get hurt.

Discuss with the team how they felt having to work as one entity. What happened if one person would not work with the others? Was there a certain amount of trust involved with the activity? Did they feel safe with the other team members holding them up and making sure they did not fall?

254. The cogs

Purpose: Learning to deal with change

Group Size: 6+

Level: Advanced

Materials: No extra materials are needed

Time: 20+ minutes

Description: The team must create a clock out of the members. Each team member is a part of the clock. When the team is ready to demonstrate the clock, they let the leader know. As it is working, the leader will tap on a team member and tell them they are no longer part of the clock. The team must work out a new plan for their clock. This is done a few times.

How did it feel to have to redesign the clock? How did it feel to be removed from the team? Was every part important?

255. No talking on the lifeline

Purpose: Problem solving, trust, and communication

Group size: 12 maximum

Level: Basic/Advanced

Materials: Duct Tape

Time: 20 minutes per each round

Description: Put down a long piece of tape on the floor. Have your team stand with their toes behind it. On your count, instruct the team to get into the tape all facing to the left. Their feet have to be on the tape; they cannot step off of it or talk while doing this exercise.

Once they are there, instruct your team to put themselves in order form oldest to youngest without stepping off the tape or talking. If anyone talks or steps off the tape, then the whole team has to start all over.

You can come up with multiple scenarios to for this game. Repeat it as many times as you think useful for your team members, and at the end discuss complications or successes that the team had as a whole or individually.

256. Cow Fence

Purpose: Teamwork

Group Size: 4+

Level: Basic

Materials: A rope and two poles or trees

Time: 10+ minutes

Description: The leader must tie the rope between the trees or poles just below waist height. This is a cow fence and cannot be touched or will sound an alarm. The team is a herd of cows making a break for freedom. They cannot touch the line in anyway and must get over the line together. Everyone in the herd should be touching the herd at all times. The herd must go over the line, not under or around. If the rules are broken the team must start over.

Did everyone work together? How many tries did it take? What was the strategy?

CREATIVE EXERCISES

257. Circle up

Purpose: Problem solving

Group size: 10+

Level: Basic

Materials: Tape

Time: 10 to 15 minutes

Description: First create multiple circles with tape on the ground in different sizes. Then ask your team to fit into any circle on the floor without anyone's feet touching space outside the tape. Once they have done so, remove two-thirds of the tape to make the circles smaller. Some people may have to find another circle to start while others stay in the original. No one's feet can touch the outside of the circle once time is called. As the leader, you can decide how much time to give your team to get themselves situated.

Keep removing tape until there is only one, large circle left that everyone has to fit into. It doesn't matter how they fit into it just as long as no one's feet touches outside of it. Start a discussion after the activity has ended about the difficulty level of working together on this task. Was it complicated? How did everyone figure out how to fit into the last circle? What did you take away from this exercise?

258. Card shuffle

Purpose: Communication and trust building

Group Size: 5+

Level: Basic

Materials: A deck of cards and a stopwatch

Time: 10+ minutes

Description: In this activity, the team leader mixes a deck of cards up. The group must get the cards in order form ace to king. The order of suits is spades, clubs, hearts, and diamonds. They have 90 seconds to do this.

Was it hard to complete? Did it take the whole team to complete? Could one person do it? Did it take a few tries to complete?

259. What's on your desk?

Purpose: Perspective

Group Size: Any

Level: Basic/Advanced

Materials: An item from each person's desk

Time: 30 minutes

Description: Ask each person to bring one item that they have sitting on their desk to the next team meeting. Tell them this is their new product for the day and that they have to come up with a slogan, logo, name and marketing plan for their object. Once time is up, give each person two minutes to present his or her product to the rest of the team. Discuss, as a team, which products everyone thinks would be the most successful and why.

This activity makes people see old objects in a new light, something that most of us forget from time-to-time. This activity can motivate your team members if they are currently stuck on a project. Instead of looking at their problem from a new angle, they can look at it from an old one instead. It also helps with problem solving and brainstorming and teaches them to think on their feet quickly.

260. Bus stop

Purpose: Teamwork and advanced problem solving

Group Size: 3+

Level: Advanced

Materials: A couple of seats to serve as a bench and paper slips with different personality traits and conflicts written on them

Time: 20 to 30 minutes (15 minutes of prep time, 20 minutes of discussion)

Description: Have the first person pick a slip of paper. On the paper are character traits and a conflict.

Example: You are a pregnant woman and need to get to the hospital. You are having contractions. Or maybe: You are an old man that is lost and forgets where he lives. You are agitated.

The situations can also be real work situations. Each person draws a slip, reads it, and then adds it to the scene. They do not let the others know what it says but act out their character instead. Each of the others must figure out a way to deal with the new situations as they arise. When everyone has had a turn, stop the scene. Make sure you discuss what you learned from the scene.

LOW COST WITH PROPS

261. Waterfall

Purpose: Teamwork and team ingenuity

Group Size: 6+

Level: Basic

Materials: Whatever is nearby. You can plant some items that can be used.

Time: 20+ minutes

Description: Mark off a 30-foot chasm on the floor or ground. Have three team members go to one side of the waterfall. These are the victims that need to be rescued. The other team members must figure out how to get across the waterfall to get to those who need to be rescued. They must use what is available to them (clothes, socks, a tree limb). They have to throw a safety line across the waterfall for victims to grab. If the line falls into the water, it must be retrieved and the team must try again. They should be able to rescue the victims one at a time.

Discuss with the team how it felt to be a victim. How did it feel to rely on others? How did the group solve the problem? Did the victims offer suggestions? Was it a team effort, or did just a couple of people take over the task? How did it feel to have limited resources?

262. Mediator

Purpose: Communication and problem solving

Group Size: 6+ (two or more groups)

Level: Advanced

Materials: Newspaper

Time: 20+ minutes

Description: The group finds a controversial subject in the newspaper. They work as a team to come up with a solution to the problem.

Here are questions that the group has to answer:

- What questions could be asked of the parties involved to work toward an agreeable solution?

- What can be changed about the situation that could prevent it from happening in the future?

- What are each side's main complaints, feelings, needs, and motivators?

- How could the problem have been averted or predicted?

- How can others in similar situations learn from this?

Give the groups a deadline. Have the groups reconvene and share their issue and how they resolved the problem by answering the five questions.
Did everyone participate in coming up with solutions? Did everyone agree on the solution? Did the group take a vote?

263. Balloon stomp

Purpose: Getting to know your team

Group size: Any

Level: First/Basic

Materials: Balloons and prepared questions

Time: 30 minutes of prep tie and 30 minutes of activity

Description: Before this activity, you will need to think of different questions and answers and put them inside each balloon. There should be enough balloons for each of your team members to stomp on.

Scatter the balloons around the room. Then invite your team members in to walk around aimlessly until you call time. Once you've called time, they are to stomp on one balloon and get out the piece of paper with either a question or answer inside. Then team members need to find the person with either the answer to their question or the question for their answer.

This activity can be used to talk about how to solve common problems at work. The questions and answers you create can be specific examples that can or have happened at work. Once everyone has found his or her partner, have him or her discuss the issue in more detail. Have each pair share what they discussed with the rest of the group to end the activity.

264. Equally Frantic

Purpose: Problem solving, listening, and communication

Group size: 10 to 20

Level: Basic

Materials: Balloons and markers

Time: 15 to 20 minutes

Description: Start the activity by asking everyone about important manner-isms to keep in mind so to treat everyone equally and fairly. Then pass out an already blown-up balloon for everyone to label. The label needs to reflect what they think it means to treat everyone in a fair, respectful manner, and it needs to be no more than four words.

Once everyone has labeled their balloon, they will toss them into the air. The goal is to keep all the balloons in the air for a certain period of time. Don't let any balloon hit the ground because every labeled balloon is important. Tell your team members they do not have to keep track of only their balloon, they should be trying to keep every balloon afloat. After 30 seconds add in more balloons for the team to keep up. If they can all keep the balloons off the group for four to five minutes then everyone earns a prize (of your choosing).

After the exercise, talk about how culture and personal identities are an important aspect of your team and why it's important to treat everyone the same despite their race, gender, or religious beliefs.

265. A shrinking vessel

Purpose: Creative problem solving

Group size: 10

Level: Basic

Materials: A rope, tape or blanket (any three will work for this activity)

Time: 15 minutes

Description: Create a large space — out of any of the three materials listed above — that your entire team can fit into comfortably. After a few seconds, make the space smaller by removing some of the material. Your team will have to rearrange themselves so they all can continue to fit in the space. As you keep shrinking the space throughout the activity, your team will continue to figure out how to fit inside. This exercise is great for your team members to practice creative problem solving and communication skills especially if you decide not to permit talking.

266. Can you count?

Purpose: Problem solving

Group Size: 8+

Level: Advanced

Materials: A deck of cards and three sheets of paper

Time: 20+ minutes

Description: Each team member is assigned a playing card. The card can be of any suit, ace through eight (more or less, depending on the size of the group). Place the sheets of paper in front of the team. They can only touch their card during the game. Have the team stack the cards from eight to ace, with the ace on top. These are stacked on one sheet of paper.

The team must restack the cards in the same order on another sheet of paper.

Here are the rules:

• Only one card can be moved at a time.

• The cards can be placed on any sheet of paper.

• A higher number card cannot be placed onto a lower number card. For example: four cannot be placed onto a three, two, or ace. However, a four can be placed onto a five, six, seven or eight.

Was this task difficult? Was it harder because everyone had to be responsible for his or her own card? What strategy did the team come up with?

267. Cut me a deal

Purpose: Communication

Group Size: 6+ (two groups)

Level: Basic

Materials: A magazine with full-page pictures, two large envelopes, and scissors

Time: 30+ minutes (10 + minutes of prep time)

Description: Take about 40 picture pages and cut them diagonally so that you have four triangles for each page. Now mix up the pieces. Put half of the pictures into each envelope. Give the envelopes to each team. Give them a few minutes to figure out what they have and what they need.

Next ask the teams to work with one another to get the pieces they need. The team that ends up with the most full pictures wins. Set a time limit.

How did negotiation go? Was everyone a part of the process? What was the strategy and who came up with it? Was a good strategy?

268. What would we look like as...

Purpose: Getting to know your team

Group Size: 4+

Level: Advanced

Materials: Different candy pieces or other objects such as board game pieces to represent each team member.

Time: 20+ minutes

Description: In this activity, team members will choose a piece of candy or whatever is available to represent them. There are different scenarios that will be presented to the team. The object is for the team to arrange the pieces so that they show how close or far away the team members are during the activities.

Here is a list of suggestions:

- A crisis on the job

- The team being rewarded for a good job

- Someone is upset (the leader can pick this person)

- A team member has messed up on the job

- A team member is leading the team (the leader can pick this person)

Each member takes a turn with each scenario to arrange the pieces on a table to represent where team members are and how close they are to other particular team members. When it is a new team member's turn, they may choose to leave the scene alone or they may move the pieces the way they see fit.

How were people's perceptions different? Were there patterns of particular people that are close? Are there team members that are always on the outside or not near anyone else? Why?

269. Fake problem

Purpose: Creative problem solving, trust, and communication

Group size: Any (but grouped in teams of four or five)

Level: Basic/Advanced

Materials: Paper and pens

Time: 30 minutes prep time and 30 minutes of participation

Description: At the beginning of your team meeting, present your staff with a fake problem or a problem that keeps reoccurring. Ask them to get into small groups of four or five and come up with a problem-solving activity to share with the rest of the group. It can be a group activity, a strategic plan, or a discussion about the importance teamwork and problem solving. Give your teams 30 minutes to hash out an idea and then 30 minutes for everyone to participate in the one you feel is best. Do not tell your team that the problem is fake until after the activity has ended. This is great practice for your team members to think creatively on their feet and handle unforeseen problems.

YOUNGER EMPLOYEES

270. Said the spider to the fly

Purpose: Strengthening teamwork and problem solving

Group Size: 6+

Level: Advanced

Materials: String. This needs to be done outdoors between two trees or poles.

Time: 20+ minutes (20+ minutes of prep time)

Description: The leader must create a web using the string. The web is tied between the two trees or poles. The holes in the web must be big enough to allow team members to crawl through without touching any string. These holes can be various sizes to add to the challenge.

The task is to get team members through the web without touching a string. Once a person makes it through a hole, the group cannot use that hole again. Everyone must make it to the other side. If someone touches a string, the whole team must start over. They can crawl between the ground and the web one time, as that counts as a hole. The web cannot be altered in any way.

How did the team work out a strategy? Was everyone important in completing this task?

271. Said the spider to the fly alternate version

Description: In this version, the team is split into two groups. This is more competitive. Each team takes turns and the rules are the same. Whenever anyone from either team goes through a hole, it is closed. The team that can get all of their members through the web first wins.

Was this harder? Was there greater strategy involved? Did the group work on a strategy together to complete the task?

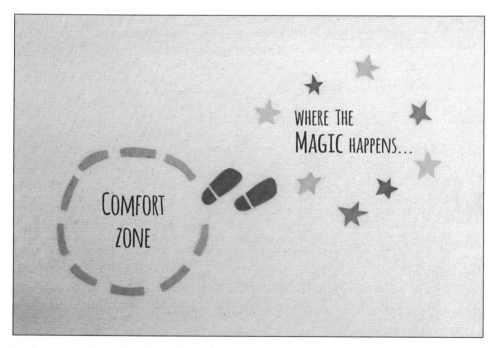

Chapter 9
Creative Thinking: Encourage Team Members to Step out of Their Comfort Zones

Team building activities bring play into the workplace. Play is the earliest method of learning, and simple group projects can help a group learn a way of thinking together.
— Michelle Lovejoy

Creative thinking is often the icing on the cake for most teams' successes. In order for your team(s) to be innovative, unique, and competitive, it's important to encourage new ways of thinking and doing. This chapter provides more team building exercises that can help team leaders alike learn about new ways to encourage and incorporate creative thinking within their teams.

IN-HOUSE TRAININGS

272. Team symbol

Purpose: Group identity development

Group Size: 4+

Level: Basic/Advanced

Materials: A lot of different magazines that can be cut up, a few pairs of scissors, paste, and a poster board

Time: 20+ minutes

Description: Each team member must cut out two pictures from the magazines. One represents the team, the other represents how the person feels about his or her role on the team. After all of the team members have found and cut out their two pictures, they should share what the pictures mean and glue it to the poster board. Each team member then adds his or her picture to the collage. The final picture is the group's symbol.

Discuss with the group how they felt about finding pictures that represented the team. Was it difficult? How do they feel about the final symbol? Is it a good representation of the entire team?

273. Team banner

Purpose: Group identity

Group Size: 4+

Level: Basic/Advanced

Materials: Paper, pens, materials to make a flag (such as felt), scissors, glue, and paint pens

Time: 30+ minutes (may need to be completed over multiple sessions)

Description: The team creates a team banner. This banner should represent the positive aspects of the group. The team should draw the banner first and color if they want to. Then the actual banner will need to be cut and decorated. When completed, the banner can be hung where all the team members can see it.

Were all the team members included in the process? Did they feel that the banner included everyone's ideas about the team? Did it help the team feel like they were a part of something important and worthwhile? How does the team feel when they see the banner hanging?

274. Code breaking

Purpose: Creative thinking and problem solving for digital teams

Group size: Any

Level: Advanced

Materials: Computer codes or cryptograms

Time: Determined by team leader

Description: This activity is meant for teams in upper management or for teams that specifically work in coding and programming. As the team leader, find a long code for your team members to break. You can split them up into smaller groups or let them work individually. You, or whoever your team leader is, determine the amount of time required to complete this activity. It could be a few minutes, a couple hours, or a few days. The team to successfully break the code first wins.

275. That's just not fair

Purpose: Learning balance

Group Size: 6+

Level: Any

Materials: Tape, balloon and a stick

Time: 15+ minutes (10 minutes of prep time)

Description: Divide the group into two groups by tallest and shortest. Tape about 30 balloons high on the wall. Give a time limit of 20 seconds. The team that can grab the most balloons in the 30 seconds wins.

How did it feel when things were not stacked in your favor? Was this unfair? Did you feel the same way when things were stacked in your favor?

COMPANY RETREATS

276. Fear in a hat

Purpose: Easing fears and open communication

Group size: Any

Level: Any

Materials: One hat, paper, and pens

Time: 30 minutes (determined by you and the size of your team)

Description: This activity works best if done before your next big team meeting or long retreat. Ask all of your team members to write down a fear they have about working for the company, being on the team, the team's projects and responsibilities, or any fear they may have that is related to work. Tell them to fold it up, keep it anonymous, and put it into the hat. Once everyone has done so take the hat and read all the fears out loud. Encourage the entire group to offer positive affirmations or suggestions after the fear has been read. As the team leader, you should be the last to speak and ease their fears — no matter what it is. This activity can give your team some peace of mind before they jump into a stressful meeting or long retreat.

277. Old barrels to sell

Purpose: Communication and creative thinking

Group Size: 6+ (at least two groups)

Level: Basic/Advanced

Materials: Paper and pens

Time: 30+ minutes

Description: This is a great activity for marketing, sales, and advertising teams. The leader states that the group has just come across 20,000 old wooden barrels and must figure out a way to market them.

The teams are given a set amount of time to come up with a plan and a pitch for the barrels. The groups come together and share their pitches. The leader chooses the most clear and concise pitch as the winner.

How hard was it to sell that many barrels? Were there creative ideas of what they could be used for or how to sell them quickly? Was it hard to come up with a sales pitch?

278. New break room

Purpose: Communication and creative thinking

Group Size: 6+ (at least two teams)

Level: Advanced

Materials: Paper and markers

Time: 20+ minutes

Description: In this activity, the groups are told that they can design a new break room. There is no budget so the sky is the limit. They are to draw it and be ready to share it with the team. The rule is that no one can talk during the activity. There should be a time limit. The team with the most complete design wins.

How did team members communicate? Was it difficult? Did they run out of time? Was it difficult not being able to talk? Did everyone agree on the design? How do you know?

279. Special report

Purpose: Communication and creative thinking

Group Size: 6+ (two teams)

Level: Advanced

Materials: Paper and pens

Time: 60+ minutes

Description: The team is split into two groups. Each must present a radio or TV special report about the other team. It should be about 15 minutes in length. They can include music, a weather report, or anything else that works in the special report. The report has to include every member of the other team. Here are some ideas for the report:

- Meteor crashes in small town

- Flood covers an island

- Family won the lottery

- Team awarded an international prize

- Lunchtime yesterday

- Team building exercises change team forever

- First team in space

The purpose is to include everyone on the other team and have updates about how they are doing on their project/work and what role they played in the report. After they create the broadcast, they should share it with the other group. Was it difficult to include everyone in the report? Did everyone on the team participate? How did the team members communicate during this exercise? Did everyone feel they were heard?

280. All tied up

Purpose: Problem solving, creativity and communication

Group size: Four to 12

Level: Basic/Advanced

Materials: String or rope

Time: 25 minutes

Description: Start with your team members facing inward in a tight circle. Then tie their wrists together with rope or string — everyone should be tied to the person next to him or her when you're finished. From here, give them a task to do together. Some examples are:

- Clean a room

- Pour a glass of water for everyone in the room

- Make a sandwich

- Organize the storage closet

Progressively make the tasks more challenging throughout the game. Take note of certain individuals' reactions during the game. Were some more easily frustrated than others? Did anyone take the role of the leader for this activity? Then discuss how this activity forced everyone to work together and problem solve as a team as opposed to completing the challenges alone. What situation could this activity relate to for your team?

281. All tied up – group walk

Description: In this version, tie your team member's ankles together instead of their wrists and give them different directions to walk in. For example, they could walk right, left, backwards, or in a circle. This version of the exercise could be more challenging and should take some time to process before each person decides to walk. You can start with smaller groups first — such as partners or groups of three — and progressively make the groups larger by adding more people to one group.

282. Build a big structure

Purpose: Creative thinking and problem solving

Group size: 10+

Level: Basic

Materials: Random materials to build a strong structure

Time: 10 minutes

Description: Split your team up into smaller groups of four or five people. They have 10 minutes to build a structure that one person can pass under. They have to make it out of the materials you brought for them. These materials can be anything from egg cartons, cereal boxes, sticky notes, duct tape, glue, pipes, markers, corks, long tubes, or plastic bags.

At the end of the allotted time, one person from each team has to go under the structure his or her team built. They cannot touch the structure nor can other team members help them get through it. Score each team on their creativity, teamwork, and will to follow directions — also, of course, if a team member could successfully pass through the structure. Whichever team has the most points at the end wins the challenge.

PHYSICAL EXERCISES

283. Human chain

Purpose: Creative thinking and problem solving

Group size: 15+

Level: Any

Materials: Paper and pens

Time: 30 minutes (10 minutes for prep)

Description: This activity works best with a large group of people; however, you can manipulate it to work with a smaller team. First, split your team into small groups of no more than eight. Then out of the eight, the group is divided into pairs

Those pairs are then given one of three roles in their team:

- Communicator (one and two)

- Observer

- Drawer

Once everyone has their role, divide them up into even spaces around the room. Draw a picture for the observers to memorize. Give them five to 10 seconds for to look at your drawing. Then, the observers will run over to communicator one and describe what they saw; communicator one then passes that information along to communicator two. He or she then runs over to the drawer's section and describes the drawing to them. The drawer's will try to match the original drawing showed to the observers. Whichever team is closest to the original drawing gets a point.

You can play as many rounds as you wish for this exercise. With each round, make the drawing harder to describe. You can also have the teams switch roles every round. So if one person were a communicator first, they would switch to drawer next and so on.

Ask questions about the team's communication strategy: Did they have one? Did it work? Or did they just wing it every time? Emphasize that the goal of the exercise was to highlight communication skills, problem solving and creative thinking skills, and communication.

284. Mirroring

Purpose: Preserving memory and creative thinking

Group size: Any

Level: Any

Materials: None

Time: 10 minutes

Description: This traditional activity is meant to strengthen your team member's memory, creative thinking skills, and non-verbal communication skills. Have your members chose a partner and stand directly across from one another. Give them each two minutes to mirror each other's actions and then switch for another two minutes.

To make the activity more interesting, set rules for each round such as:

- Stand on one leg

- Make eye contact the whole

- Do not use your right arm

This will make the exercise more challenging and fun for your team members.

285. No man's land

Purpose: Problem solving and time management

Group size: Any

Level: Any

Materials: Masking tape, carrier bag, a yardstick, a container large enough to hold 10 tennis balls, and other random supplies (to be discussed below)

Time: 25 minutes (including prep time)

Description: Tape two parallel lines on the floor about five feet apart. One is the start line and the other is the finish line. The space in between is No Man's Land. Set a container of tennis balls behind the starting line and another container full of random supplies that your team can use to push the tennis balls across the finish line.

Some examples are:

- Index cards

- Deflated balloons

- Straw

- Paper plates

- Tape

- Scissors

- String

- Paper clips

The goal is for the team to get every tennis ball across the finish line using the resources they were provided. They have 10 minutes to complete the challenge and cannot step into No Man's Land at any point in time. Divide your team up into two teams to make it a friendly competition.

286. Lava Flow

Purpose: Communication and teamwork

Group size: Any

Level: Any

Materials: Materials for people to step on (pieces of paper, carpet squares, crates, etc.), blindfolds and rope

Time: 25 to 30 minutes

Description: Mark off a space with the rope — this is the "volcano." Spread out the materials you brought for people to step on inside the marked off area and then split your team up into two groups.

One at a time, each team member will cross the lava blindfolded. Only team members who made it successfully across get to shout directions to his or her teammate crossing over next. Anyone who steps into the lava is out. The team with most players remaining at the end wins the game. The first person to go has the most challenging job because he or she does not have anyone on the other side directing them.

287. Traffic jam

Purpose: Creative thinking and communication

Group size: Any

Level: Any

Materials: Cones

Time: 55 minutes

Description: First split your team into team teams — Team A and Team B. Line them up vertically facing each other with A facing B and vice-versa. Put a cone in between each partner. The goal of the game is to get side A to side B and side B to side A all facing forward.

The rules are as follows:

1. No moving backward

2. Team members cannot jump over one another

3. Only one person can move at a time

4. One spot per person, no sharing!

5. If any of these rules are broken, everyone has to start all over

This exercise may take some time, so plan accordingly. Observe your team members for patience and cooperation, and at the end of the activity discuss who stood out to you most with these qualities. Ask what was difficult about this challenge and why.

CREATIVE EXERCISES

288. Fix it

Purpose: Communication

Group Size: 4+

Level: Any

Materials: Blocks and a stopwatch

Time: 15+ minutes

Description: The leader will stack the blocks in a random way on the table and announce that the team will have to "fix" the stack in 60 seconds. The leader will say, "Go." The team will have to interpret what "fix" means. If they ask the leader for clarification, the leader will only repeat the instructions.

Would this be easier if you had better instructions? Did the team give up? Did the team develop a quick strategy?

289. Fix it alternate version

Description: Instead of blocks, the leader will hand the group a page-long excerpt from a magazine, paper, or newsletter. The instruction will be the same:

"Fix it." The leader can add spelling or grammatical errors to the passage to help the process.

Was it hard to find what was wrong with the passage? Did the team choose what to do? Did one person make corrections or was it a group effort?

290. One person's trash is another person's treasure

Purpose: Team creativity

Group Size: 4+ (at least two groups will be formed)

Level: Basic

Materials: Glue, scissors, and any material that would be discarded such as paper towel rolls, string, newspaper, cans, jars, bottles, or magazines

Time: 20+ minutes

Description: The groups are given a pile of "trash" and use the items to create a masterpiece. Each member of the group must pick an item to add to the piece. When everyone has completed the task, there can be an art show. Each group must describe their art piece.

The leader should ask how it felt to work with others in a creative setting. Was it hard to share and allow others to add to the art piece? Were people surprised by others' creative skills? How was the decision made about what to build and how to build it?

291. Create a design

Purpose: Communication and creative thinking

Group Size: 4+ divided into pairs

Level: Basic

Materials: Legos — you need enough for each member of the team. You need to have the same pieces for each person. Ten or fewer pieces are suggested.

Time: 10 to 30 minutes (prep time of 10 minutes to sort Legos into piles for each team member)

Description: Partners sit with their backs to each other so they cannot see what the other is doing. Each person is given a set of identical Legos. Partner A creates a design on the table/floor and describes the design to Partner B. The first time this is done, Partner B cannot ask any questions of Partner A. The roles are reversed and the same thing is done. Then, the activity is repeated for each pair and this time the person receiving the directions can ask questions.

292. Team shield

Purpose: Creative thinking

Group size: Any

Level: First/Basic

Materials: Cardboard, paper, markers, glue, and colored pencils

Time: 20 minutes

Description: Split your team up into smaller groups and have them create a team shield out of the materials you supplied. The shield should represent the entire team's identity. To incorporate more communication, have each person draw a shield first, and then when groups are formed they can choose one thing from each person's drawing to make one large one. When each team is finished, have them present their shield to the rest of the group. Put them on display in the break room or a team space so everyone remembers what your team stands for.

LOW COST WITH PROPS

293. Human shapes

Purpose: Creative thinking and teamwork

Group size: Four to 20

Level: First/Basic

Materials: None

Time: 20 minutes

Description: As a team, ask your members to form letters and words with their bodies. Start off with letters first. Making one letter won't need more than three people, so make sure everyone has a turn before you start calling out words for them to try. Once everyone has gotten the hang of making words, give the group a sentence that everyone has to be a part of making. This activity is fun to do after a longer, more serious exercise. It's great for new teams, too.

294. Balloon keep-up

Purpose: Communication and teamwork

Group size: 8+

Level: First

Materials: Balloons

Time: 15 minutes (five per round)

Description: Blow up a pack of balloons and toss them into the air for your team players to keep up in the air. They are only allowed to touch a balloon one time before the hit a different one. If anyone hits a balloon more than once then they are taken out of the game. Play three rounds and keep adding in more balloons each time. This is light exercise that is great for teams that just met.

295. Paper plane contest

Purpose: Collaboration and creative thinking skills

Group size: Any

Level: First (but any level can play)

Materials: Tape, cardstock, and a measuring stick (ruler or yardstick)

Time: 15 minutes

Description: Split your team into smaller groups and give them each cardstock and a list of different airplane models to create. They are to choose the one they think will fly the farthest. Give them 10 minutes to construct a paper airplane. After the 10 minutes is up, create a starting point with tape on the floor and have each team test their planes from there. Whichever team's plane gets the farthest wins the challenge.

Chapter 10
Think Positive Thoughts: Activities That Will Spread Positivity from Employee to Employee

One of the most important factors of a team's success is each member's behavior and attitude toward the team, the company, and team projects. Thinking positive and remaining positive at work is one way to accomplish such a task.

Individuals who possess a positive mindset and realize their self actualization on a team make for more healthy, hardworking teammates. Teams that are self-actualized are often pleasant and have a positive outlook on work and life in general. They embrace the values and ethics of the team. They act according to what is right, regardless of what authorities may demand. They have a highly developed sense of what is right.

This chapter gives you multiple team building exercises that focus on channeling positivity through your team and from teammate to teammate. The activities can be used for both new and old teams; however, some require a large amount of patience, honesty, and the will to dig deeper into understanding one another. Teams that have been working together for longer periods of time may benefit more from these kinds of exercises as opposed to newly formed teams because they are more willing to fulfill such requirements. However, it doesn't mean new teams cannot try such activities. Change them as you much as you need to so your team members can have similar experiences to older teams and bond in a similar way.

IN-HOUSE TRAININGS

296. Share a defining moment

Purpose: Team support and positivity

Group size: Any

Level: Any

Materials: None

Time: 25 minutes

Description: This activity is simple and can be completed at your next team meeting or lunch outing. Go around the room and have each person share a defining moment in their life. It could be getting a job, getting fired, having children, or something random like switching majors — anything that that person thinks helped shaped them into the person they are today. This will help your team members get to know a deeper side of one another despite how long they have worked together.

297. Hero, highlight, hardship

Purpose: Team support and positivity

Group size: Any

Level: Any

Materials: None

Time: 25 minutes

Description: This activity is similar to the one above but team members are sharing both positive and negative memories from their past this time. Go around the room and have each person share who their hero is and why, along with a life highlight and hardship. These do not have to be work related. Make sure everyone is encouraging and supportive throughput the entire exercise. This behavior will make everyone feel as comfortable as possible when he or she takes a turn to speak.

298. The votes are in

Purpose: Team morale booster

Group Size: 5+

Level: Advanced

Materials: Pen and paper

Time: 30+ minutes

Description: Each team member writes a speech about why they should be voted onto the team. This speech should include their positive traits and what they can do for the team. This should be short (about a page). When everyone is finished, they should read their speech to the team and everyone should applaud when they have finished.

How did it feel to be applauded for? How did it feel to write nice things about yourself and keep it strengths based?

299. If you really knew me

Purpose: Team morale booster support

Group size: Any

Level: Advanced

Materials: Paper and pens

Time: 30 minutes

Description: Have each team member fill in the blank to this statement: "If you really knew me, you would know _____." At first, your team members' responses may seem a little vague, shy, or even narcissistic. But after playing two or three rounds their responses will get deeper.

Give guidelines for them to follow for each round. In round one, only give your team members the sentence; for round two, ask them to answer the statement with a positive event, trait, or quality that they have or have experienced; and for round three, ask them to dig a little deeper and answer with something they normally would not share with their coworkers. Remember, good employees follow great leaders, so don't forget to share deep experiences with your employees — it will make them feel more comfortable before they take their turn. This exercise will bring your members closer together, especially if a big event or project is approaching.

300. Fuel up the tanks

Purpose: Team morale booster and support

Group size: Any

Level: Advanced

Materials: Manila envelopes and index cards

Time: On-going

Description: This exercise is to be thought of as a source of positive energy that is always running through your workplace. Give each of your employees or team members a manila envelope with a picture of a bus and their name on it (or any positive image that you think resembles your team). This envelope resembles their energy bus tank.

Before and after every team project, event, or deadline, have each employee write something positive about one of his or her teammates on an index card and put it into his or her envelope. They can write positive thoughts, words of encouragement, or accomplishments on the cards.

Keep the envelopes in an area that's accessible for everyone so they can reach into their energy bus tanks and read their cards whenever they need to do so. This type of interaction can increase communication and team support before and after every major event that the team has to face together, even if the outcome is negative. Don't forget to participate in this activity yourself if you are a team leader. Hearing positive thoughts from upper management can really improve your team's overall motivation and behavior because their hard work is being noticed.

301. Winner-loser

Purpose: Maintaining a positive mindset

Group size: Any

Level: Basic/Advanced

Materials: None

Time: 10 minutes (for both players)

Description: Split your team up into pairs — partner A and partner B. Give them each 10 minutes to share something negative that has happened to them at work, because of work or in life in general. Then the opposite partner is to focus on what the positives could be for his or her partner for the situation he or she just shared. For example, when partner A shares his or her negative experience with partner B, then partner B needs to discuss the positive aspects of the situation to help his or her partner see the situation from a new angle. This exercise will help team members learn how to reframe negative situations into positive ones together, instead of on their own.

302. Who wants a job?

Purpose: Understanding leadership traits

Group Size: 6+

Level: Basic

Materials: Blank employment forms

Time: 20+ minutes

Description: Each team member must fill out an application. The task is to pick a great leader in history and pretend that the leader is the one filling out the application. The important areas are strengths and past experiences. Each team member states strengths and experiences that his or her person has. The first person to figure out who the leader is wins a point. This continues through the group. The person with the most points wins.

What characteristics were common between the various people that were great leaders? What defined them as great?

303. Who wants a job alternate version

Description: In this version, the team members fill out their own applications. Their names and other obvious identifying information are not included. The applications are handed around the group. The team members guess who they are. The leader reads them out loud, and the person whose application it is raises his or her hand. The team member with the most correct guesses wins.

Was it hard to recognize other people by their strengths? Was it hard to fill out your own application knowing other team members would read it?

304. Climate checker

Purpose: Identifying and addressing team issues

Group size: 6+

Level: Advanced

Materials: Flip chart paper or a whiteboard and markers

Time: Five minutes per topic

Description: On large paper or a whiteboard draw a scale from one to 10 (one being strongly disagree and 10 being strongly agree). Then write a statement above the scale that addresses a particular topic or issue in your workplace. It could be something simple such as, "I think we work well as a team," or something more controversial that needs to be addressed. Your team members will then vote on the statement you wrote. Hand out markers for them to mark an X on the scale that will show how they feel about that statement. Take time to review and calmly discuss the results of each statement with your team. Repeat the process with as many topics you feel need to be addressed with your team.

305. Skill hunt

Purpose: Getting to know your team

Group Size: 4+

Level: Advanced

Materials: Pens and paper

Time: 15+ minutes

Description: The leader will instruct each team member to write down any positive skill or trait that he or she brings to the team. When the team members have completed their lists, they must hunt down other people and look at their lists. They are to write down skills from other people's lists that are not contained on their own. They are given five minutes per four people. The person with the most unique skills and positive traits listed on his or her paper wins.

306. Me and my shadow

Purpose: Team morale booster

Group Size: 5+

Level: Basic

Materials: Paper and colored pens

Time: 10+ minutes

Description: Have each team member draw his or her shadow on the piece of paper. This is basically a body outline. Now have each team member label the different parts of his or her shadow with positive attributes like:

- **Head:** good thinker

- **Legs:** good dancer

- **Eyes:** can see problems clearly

- **Mouth:** words of encouragement for others

Have the team members share their shadows with the group. Was it hard for them to think of positive aspects? Did they see themselves differently? Did they agree with what was written on other people's shadows?

307. Me and my shadow alternate version

Description: In this version, everyone on the team fills in the different body parts on each other's shadows. The shadows should be labeled and passed to the left for one minute before being passed to the next person until everyone has had a chance to write on each.

How did people feel about what their team members wrote? Would they agree with other people's assessments of them? Did they learn about new strengths in themselves?

308. Superheroes

Purpose: Team morale booster

Group Size: 6+ (at least two teams)

Level: Advanced

Materials: Paper and pens

Time: 20+ minutes

Description: Each group is assigned to create a story in which all members of the other team are included. Each character has a superpower that correlates to a skill he or she brings to the group.

- *Here is a list of examples:*
- Supportive = super strength
- Fast worker = super speed
- Foundation of the group = can turn themselves into stone
- Can see a problem and fix it = super sight

The story they create is about the members of the other group using their superpowers to beat the bad guys. The stories are shared at the end with the other group. The leader should explore how it felt to be a superhero. Were the superpowers chosen the same powers that the people would have chosen themselves? Was anyone surprised about his or her superpower?

309. Superheroes alternate version

Description: In this version, a comic book is created about the group. This works well with an artistic team. The team members must give the team a superhero team name. They must create names for the superheroes according to their superpower and they must create costumes for the superheroes.

310. Team obituary

Purpose: Creating team identity

Group Size: 6+

Level: Basic/Advanced

Materials: Paper and pens

Time: 20+ minutes

Description: The team must write an obituary for the team. It should include all of the team members and their accomplishments. It should include all of the great things the team did and why the team will be missed. This is a great activity for teams who are close to finishing their projects.

Were their items included that the team has not done yet? Were only team members' strengths mentioned or were team struggles mentioned as well?

COMPANY RETREATS

311. Destruction of property

Purpose: Team morale booster

Group Size: 4+

Level: Advanced

Materials: Different color spray paint cans, paint masks, a large piece of butcher paper, or an old white bed sheet. This activity should be done outdoors on a day that is not windy, and team members should wear old clothes.

Time: 20+ minutes (10 minutes of prep time)

Description: The team will make creative graffiti. They are to spray paint the sheet and write people's names and something positive about them. They can be as creative as they want. The sheet can be on the ground or hung on a wall. Make sure the paint will not get on any important structure. Set grounds rules for safety with the group. Make sure the painting dries before touching or moving it.

How did team members feel about seeing their names with positive traits around it? Did the activity bring the team members closer together?

312. Destruction of property alternate version

Description: In this version, the team paints logos and words about the team rather than individuals. They should use words that promote positive aspects of the team.

313. What's in your bag?

Purpose: Getting to know your team

Group Size: 4+

Level: Advanced

Materials: Paper lunch sacks, a pile of different magazines and newspapers, glue, and scissors for each team member

Time: 30+ minutes

Description: The team must do two different things. The first task is to find pictures in the magazines that reflect how the team members think others see them. These are to be glued on the outside. On the inside of the bag they must put pictures that reflect how the individuals see themselves.

How were the two sets of pictures different? Was anyone surprised by another person's bag?

314. Personal scrapbook

Purpose: Team bonding

Group Size: 4+

Level: Advanced

Materials: Paper, pens and markers

Time: 20+ minutes

Description: Give each team member a stack of eight to 10 pages. Give them a list of what should be on each page. They are to create pages of their personal scrapbook. They can color and decorate them if they wish. When they have completed the task, they should share their book with other members of the team.

Here is a list of possible pages in the books:

- Favorite book

- Favorite movie

- Favorite food

- Where did you grow up?

- Where did you go to school?

- What was your saddest moment?

- What was your happiest moment?

- What was your most embarrassing moment?

- What did people learn about their teammates? Was it hard to share personal information?

315. Team scrapbook

Description: In this version, the team creates a book that represents the group. Each page contains a different team member and information about them. The book can be shared with new team members and pages can be added for them. How did the group feel about creating the book together? Did they like having their own pages? Did they ask others to help them with their pages?

316. The judges say

Purpose: Identifying your team role

Group Size: 6+

Level: Advanced

Materials: No extra materials are needed

Time: 20+ minutes

Description: Each team member is asked to think of four reasons that the team needs him or her. Each team member must yell, scream, dance, or do whatever it takes to convince their peers that he or she should be a member. The team leader and other team members will judge them. Humor, loudness, and originality are all factors. The team should give them a rating from one to 10. The team member with the most points wins.

How did it feel to convince the team about your role as a team member? Was it hard to come up with good reasons? What did you think of other people's reasons?

317. Give a compliment

Purpose: Spread positivity and team bonding

Group size: Any

Level: Advanced

Materials: Technology that's capable of filming video i.e. — a smartphone, laptop, or tablet

Time: 60 minutes

Description: This activity works best with a team that has been working together for a longer period of time, but it can be used with newer teams, too.

To start, have every team member draw one of their coworkers' names out of a hat. They are to film a short video message for that person discussing the positive attributes he or she brings to the team. It can be sentimental, funny, or happy. Ask your team to email their video clips to the team leader so he or she can edit them all together to make a presentation. At the next big team meeting have the team leader share the presentation. It'll be a nice surprise for everyone to hear what he or she means to someone else, especially if they have a weak relationship. This exercise can help strengthen the team's bond as well as bonds between two people.

318. The 'glad' game

Purpose: Maintaining a positive mindset

Group size: Any

Level: Advanced

Materials: None

Time: 20 minutes

Description: Split your team up into pairs or small groups of three or four. They are to each take a turn and share a negative experience with each other. In turn, those who are listening should respond with a positive thought that could come out of the negative experience.

For example, team member one shares that she got demoted in her department. The other players should respond with something positive such as "Yes, you got demoted by now you have more time to focus on yourself" or "you have more time to spend with your family." The idea is for the team to help each other find something they need to be "glad" about despite experiencing something so negative.

PHYSICAL EXERCISES

319. Self-esteem pillow sheets

Purpose: Self-esteem booster

Group Size: 6+

Level: Basic

Materials: Pillowcase and a small softball

Time: 10+ minutes

Description: The leader holds the pillowcase open on one side of the room. The team lines up on the other side and takes turns trying to get the ball into the pillowcase. If they make the shot, they must say something nice or positive about themselves. If they miss the shot they must pick someone else to try and say something nice about them. If the team members make the shot, they continue to throw the ball until they miss.

How did it feel to say nice things about yourself? How did it feel to have someone else say nice things to you?

320. Self-esteem pillow sheets alternate version

Description: In this version, the foam-core board has three holes cut into it. It is propped up so beanbags can be thrown into the holes. At each hole, the person must do something different.

An example is:

Hole one: Say something nice about yourself.

Hole two: Say something nice about yourself and get a piece of candy.

Hole three: Say something nice about yourself and give a piece of candy to someone else.

If the person misses, they must pass the beanbag and say something nice about the next person.

Did anyone try for the third hole? Why or why not? Did they try harder for hole one or hole two? Why?

321. Tap me next

Purpose: Team morale booster

Group Size: 6+

Level: Advanced

Materials: No extra materials are needed

Time: 20+ minutes (10 + minutes of prep time)

Description: The leader creates a list of positive affirmations that team members can identify with.

Here is a sample list:

- A person who makes me smile

- A person who makes me laugh

- A person I trust

- A person I admire

- A person who is a hard worker

The leader asks one person to stand up. The rest of the team lies down their heads. The leader reads one of the affirmations. The person standing picks a person who fits this description. The chosen person stands and joins the first person. The leader reads another one and those standing pick one person each who fits that description until everyone is eventually standing. A new person is chosen to start and the game can be repeated using new affirmations.

How did it feel to be chosen for a particular affirmation? Did you have any difficulty finding someone who fit a particular affirmation?

322. Hunting for happiness

Purpose: Team positivity

Group size: Any

Level: Any

Materials: Random materials suggested by your team members (explained below)

Time: 30 minutes

Description: If your team is feeling a little sluggish lately, use this activity to get them more motivated at work. Send out a short survey asking them what small objects make them happy. This can be a gift card for $5 or $10, office supplies, or even their favorite singer's poster. Once you've gathered everyone's responses, create a happiness scavenger hunt for your employees to participate in. They can go around the office and find materials just for them or items meant for the team as a whole. Do this activity on a day when most people are present such as after lunch or at the beginning of the week.

CREATIVE EXERCISES

323. Queen for a day

Purpose: Team morale booster

Group Size: 3+

Level: Advanced

Materials: A chair/throne, a crown, treasures such as candies or small toy items, paper and pens

Time: 30+ minutes (some prep time may be needed if you create a crown or decorate the throne)

Description: Each person must write something nice about every member on the team. The compliments should be short and simple.

Team members take turns sitting in the throne. They put on the crown. The other team member bows says something nice about the royal person and leaves him or her a small gift. Each person should have time on the throne.

How did the team members feel about being on throne? How did they feel about bowing and bringing a team member a gift? Did this exercise make team members feel good about themselves?

324. Personal advertisements

Purpose: Team morale booster

Group Size: 4+

Level: Advanced

Materials: Poster, markers, crayons, and paints

Time: 20+ minutes

Description: In this exercise, the team will each be given a poster. They must create a bright and colorful poster that advertises them. It should say what their positive attributes are and contain pictures or scenes that reflect that person. The posters should be hung up as a reminder of people's strengths.

How did people feel about creating a personal advertisement? Was it hard to create something positive about themselves?

325. Personal advertisements alternate version

Description: In this version, the focus of the advertisements should be about the team and the team's strengths. This can be an individual project or the team can create one together.

How did people feel about writing positive things about the team? Did everyone say the same things or did people write different strengths?

326. Newspaper ads

Purpose: Team morale booster

Group Size: 4+

Level: Advanced

Materials: Paper and pens

Time: 15+ minutes

Description: In a paragraph or less, a person should write a personal ad. It should describe positive attributes and strengths.

The paragraphs are written anonymously. The leader should read them aloud and allow the team to guess whose personal ads they are.

How did the team members feel about advertising themselves for a team to hire? Did they feel it was hard to sell their positive attributes? Was a paragraph too much or too limiting?

327. Newspaper ads alternate version

Description: In this version, the group will create an ad about the team to try to sell the team to a company. It should include positive attributes about the team and its members and should be limited to two paragraphs.

Did everyone participate? Did everyone feel they had input in the ad? Would they hire a team with that kind of advertisement? Why or why not?

328. Personal stamps

Purpose: Getting to know your team

Group Size: 4+

Level: Advanced

Materials: Paper, pens, and colored markers

Time: 15+ minutes

Description: Team members create postage stamps that represent them. The stamps should have a picture and a word that represents who they are on the team. The team members should share their stamps with others.

How did the team members feel about reducing themselves to postage stamp size? Was this hard to do? Was it too limiting?

329. Tree of plenty

Purpose: Team morale building

Group Size: 5+

Level: Basic

Materials: Construction paper (brown, white, and green), pens, and glue

Time: 10+ minutes

Description: Each person should cut out a trunk of the tree. Green leaves are cut out for each team member to write on. They should glue their trunk onto the white paper. On the trunk they should write a talent that they bring to the team. They are to put their names on the leaves on one side and then the teams should send their leaves for other team members to write one talent that the person brings to the team. Each team member gathers his or her leaves and glues them onto the trunk, which creates a tree of talent. The group should share their trees.

The group should discuss if there were any duplicate leaves. Did they learn about any talents they did not know they had?

330. Group résumé

Purpose: Team bonding

Group size: Four to five per group

Level: Basic

Materials: Flip chart paper and markers

Time: 30 minutes

Description: Before beginning this exercise, talk about the array of talents and skill sets each team member already brings to the team. Discuss how important each individual is to the team and why. From there, divide your group into smaller teams with about four to five people in each. In these groups, they will make a group resume on a piece of flip-chart paper.

Ask them to include the following:

- Education background

- Professional experience

- Professional skills and qualifications

- Major achievements

- Hobbies, travel, family, volunteer experience, etc.

Encourage them to get creative about how they are going to incorporate everyone's experiences and skill sets into the group resume. Give them about 20 to 25 minutes to complete the activity and then invite each group to share what they came up with at the end. After the exercise is over, take some time to debrief and talk about what they all learned about each other. Ask them what skills they think will come in handy from certain people as the team takes on larger projects and events in the future.

LOW COST WITH PROPS

331. Secret admirer

Purpose: Getting to know your team

Group Size: 4+

Level: Advanced

Materials: Pens, envelopes, and enough slips of paper for each team member to make a comment about every other team member. Here is an example for a team of four members:

3 for each person x 4 people = 12 slips of paper

Time: 20+ minutes

Description: Each person will receive an envelope with slips of paper and should write his or her name on the envelope. The envelopes should be passed to the left. Each team member should write one nice thing about the person whose envelope they have on the slip of paper.

When they are finished, they are to put the slip of paper back into the envelope. The envelopes are then passed to the left and the procedure is repeated. When everyone has had a turn, the team leader will collect the envelopes. He or she will call a person to the front, and they will pull the slips of paper out and read them individually. The person must guess whom the secret admirer is that wrote the comment on the slip. This is repeated for each team member.

The leader should discuss how the team felt getting positive comments from other team members. How did it feel when it was revealed that you wrote the comment? Would they have preferred it remained anonymous? How did it feel to know that other team members had such high esteem for them?

332. One step into the future

Purpose: Getting to know your team

Group Size: 4+

Level: Advanced

Materials: Paper, pens, and markers

Time: 10+ minutes

Description: Each person traces his or her foot onto the paper and colors or decorates the foot. It must include the person's name and one goal he or she hopes to accomplish in the next five years. The team will then share their feet with other team members.

How did it feel to share private goals with the team? Can team members help them achieve the goal?

333. One step into the future alternate version

Description: In this version, the team creates feet to represent goals they would like the team to achieve in the next year or two. This can be done on a large poster board where everyone traces his or her feet.

Can the team accomplish these goals together? Are they similar to people's personal goals?

334. Crystal ball

Purpose: Getting to know your team

Group Size: 4+

Level: Advanced

Materials: Paper and pens

Time: 20+ minutes

Description: In this activity, each team member will fold his or her paper into four sections. The team members are to put their names on the paper.

In each of the four sections, write one of these four headings:

- 1 year
- 2 years
- 5 years
- 20 years

Once this is completed, have everyone pass his or her paper to the right. They will write something about where they see that particular person in each of the four time frames. The paper is passed again and the procedure is repeated. Continue this until each person has his or her original paper back.

How did you feel about the predictions? Did you agree? Do people really understand you and your goals in life? Do you want to tell others whether they are right or wrong? Did this exercise make you feel good or bad?

335. Flipping great

Purpose: Ensuring team positivity

Group size: Any

Level: Basic/Advanced

Materials: Flip chart paper, pens and tacks or tape

Time: 20 to 30 minutes

Description: Give each team member a piece of flip chart paper with his or her name on the top. Ask them to tape or pin the piece of paper up around the room. Then explain that each person will go around the room and write one positive attribute or message about that person on his or her piece of paper.

Sentences or phrases cannot be repeated, so everyone must come up with something new on each paper. At the end of the exercise, invite team members to share about what their coworkers wrote about them.

Were they surprised to see some of the messages on their paper? Did any stand out to them more than others? What did they think about the activity? Encourage them to leave these papers in their offices to look back on when things start to pile up or get tough.

BREATHING EXERCISES

Below are a few simple breathing techniques that could be useful for teams that are under a lot of pressure. According to the American Institute of Stress, focused breathing helps relax the body and reduce stress. It also helps lower anxiety, which could be a serious health disorder that your employees or teammates suffer from periodically due to large projects and looming deadlines. To avoid anxiety or to help lower stress, try implementing a de-stress session at work and use one of the breathing techniques below.

336. Take a breath exercise one

Purpose: Relaxation

Group Size: 3+

Level: Any

Materials: None

Time: 10+ minutes

Description: Have the team members sit in a comfortable way. The leader will talk the group through the breathing exercise.

1. Inhale through your nose. Do this slowly over the count of five. One, two, three, four, five. An inhalation should be inflating your lungs. Filling them with life-giving oxygen. You have a muscle at the bottom of lungs called the diaphragm. When you inhale, this muscle pulls down. This action draws air inside the lungs. Your lungs expand like balloons. They push everything, including your lungs and organs aside. So when you take a deep breath hold your hand lightly over your stomach, just below the ribcage. As your lungs inhale you should feel them push against your hand. When you reach the count of five your lungs should be as inflated as is comfortably possible.

2. Now exhale through your mouth. Do this over the count of five. When you exhale, toxic gases are expelled from your body. Make sure all of it is gone. When you exhale, your diaphragm is pushing upward literally pushing the air out of you. Your lungs deflate. All of your organs and ribs return to their normal state. All of the bad feelings and thoughts have gone.

3. Repeat the process. Breathe in through your nose. One, two, three, four, five.

4. Breathe out from your mouth. One, two, three, four, five.

5. Repeat one more breath in, then out.

Did you feel more relaxed after the exercise? Can this help as a daily exercise? Can it help focus our thoughts and emotions?

337. Take a breath exercise two

Description: This breathing exercise is slightly more advanced. It should not be attempted with the team until they have mastered the previous breathing exercise.

1. Sit in a comfortable quiet place. Make sure you will not be disturbed. Inhale through your nose. Do this slowly over the count of five. One, two, three, four, five. Breath should be inflating your lungs.

2. This time, hold your breath in for the count of three. One, two, three. You are allowing the body longer to absorb the oxygen you have just breathed in. It also is signaling the mind to relax the muscles.

3. Now exhale through your mouth. Do this over the count of five. One, two, three, four, five.

4. When you exhale toxic thoughts and emotions are expelled from your body. Make sure all of it is gone.

5. This time hold your breath out for a count of three. One, two, three.

6. Inhale through your nose. One, two, three, four, five.

7. Hold for three. One, two, three.

8. Exhale for five. One, two, three, four, five.

9. Repeat one more controlled breath. Inhale. Hold. Exhale. Hold.

10. Return to normal breathing.

338. Take a breath exercise three

Description: This exercise is the next incarnation of the breathing exercise. Each advanced version builds upon the prior exercise.

1. This time, you will use your finger to pinch one nostril close. Start with your right nostril. Use your thumb and gently push it closed. Inhale through your left nostril. One, two, three, four, five.

2. Hold your breath for three. One, two, three.

3. Exhale through your mouth. One, two, three, four, five.

4. Hold your breath. One, two, three.

5. Take your thumb and pinch your left nostril now. Inhale through your right nostril. One, two, three, four, five.

6. Hold for three. One, two, three.

7. Exhale through your mouth. One, two, three, four, five.

8. Hold for three. One, two, three.

9. Now cover your right nostril again and repeat the exercise with steps one through eight two more times.

10. Return to normal breathing.

339. Black board

Purpose: Focus

Group Size: 3+

Level: Advanced

Materials: None

Time: 10+ minutes

Description: Team members sit in a comfortable way. The team leader leads the exercise.

1.   Find a comfortable chair or place where it is quiet and you will not be disturbed.

2.   Breathe as you have learned. Breathe in through your nose. One, two, three, four, five.

3.   Hold for three. Exhale through your mouth. One, two, three, four, five. Hold for three. Do this breathing two more times.

4.   Close your eyes. Now imagine you are sitting alone in a classroom. You are completely alone. You are sitting in a comfortable chair and right in front of you is the largest, black chalkboard you have ever seen. It is clean and blank. On the desk are two items, a piece of chalk and an eraser.

5.   Spend a few moments and look at the blackboard. There is nothing there. It is just blank.

6.   You will begin to notice thoughts creeping into your mind. They can be anything: "Boy, I'm hungry;" "I wonder what Jane is doing right now;" "I am so glad I bought this book." As these thoughts come to mind, begin to write them on the board before you. One after the other, write down these thoughts.

Fill the board with your "mind-speak." Do not judge the thoughts — just write them down. Fill the entire board until no more thoughts will fit.

7.   Take your eraser and begin to erase all of these thoughts. If a thought creeps back into your mind, you have to write it on the board and then erase it again. Keep erasing until you are back to the blackboard.

8. Now the board is black, blank, and empty.

9. Hold this blackboard as long as you can with nothing else in your mind.

10. When you are ready open your eyes.

How did the exercise make you feel? Are you more focused? Did it help relax you? Can this exercise help when things are busy and stressful?

340. Sweep it away

Purpose: Team morale booster

Group Size: 3+

Level: Advanced

Materials: None

Time: 10+ minutes

Description: Have the team members sit in a comfortable place in the room. Directions are below:

1. Close your eyes. Remember to be alert and try not to fall asleep.

2. Clear your mind. Now in your mind, picture the worst moment you have experienced while working on the team. This is a time when teamwork was lacking. The important thing is that it needs to be clear in your mind. You have to see it, hear it, and smell it.

See the faces of the people on your team and get a good picture of their expressions. Make this entire scene fill your mind and make sure it is vivid and clear. You should feel anxious and uncomfortable. Capture how you felt when this incident occurred. When the image is sharp and clear, you should feel that anxiety.

Once you have achieved this, take a color picture of it in your mind. Label this picture your "worst team moment." Make sure you give it this label, as it will make it easier to recall it later. Now set aside this picture in your mind. Take a few deep breaths and move to the next step.

3. Clear your mind again. This time, imagine you dealt with a difficult situation successfully. You felt confident and the team was working together successfully in the face of a challenge. Like the previous step, make it clear and sharp in your mind.

Hear it, smell it, see it, and feel it. See the faces around you smiling. Hear their praises of one another. Feel them tapping you on the back and shaking your hand. Feel that sense of self-worth and confidence welling up inside you. Once you feel this elation take a color snapshot in your mind. Label this one "the moment of team success."

Let the scene start to fade slowly. The colors are running out of the picture and it turns to black and white. The picture will now begin to shrink smaller and smaller to about the size of a postage stamp. Lay this tiny "moment of team success" aside.

4. Take a moment. Pick up that "worst team moment."

5. Make it clear in your mind again. Make it clear and vivid enough to make you feel that uncomfortable anxiety. This time in the bottom left corner is the "moment of team success." It should look like the picture on a television where the screen is the large picture of a show, while in the corner is a small picture of another show playing on a different channel.

6. Once you have the image of the two pictures say, "Sweep." As you do this, the pictures change. The "moment of team success" picture trades places with the "worst team moment" picture. The "worst team moment" is now that tiny postage stamp. Enjoy and feel the elation of the "moment of team success" for a time.

7. Say "Sweep" again and switch the "moment of team success" with the "worst team moment." The "moment of team success" becomes small again but stays in the picture. Feel the anxiety of the "worst team moment." Say "Sweep." Now, quickly switch back to the "moment of team success" again.

8. Repeat step seven five more times.

9. Now let your mind drift to a neutral place. It could be a park, a room, a beach, or anywhere you are comfortable and at ease.

It is important that you do not skip this step. Enjoy your neutral spot for a few moments and then open your eyes. You are done.

How did this feel? Would it be worth trying this by yourself daily? Can it help the team feel more confident and overcome failures?

Chapter 11
Technology: Team Building Activities for Remote Teams

In today's working economy, a lot of people have the opportunity to work from home because the advances in technology allow them to do so. Technology makes it easy for self-employed or remote employees to communicate with colleagues and stay on task. According to Global Workplace Analytics, about 3.7 million U.S. employees' work from home at least part-time and 22 percent of that number includes the self-employed population, too.

To accommodate the rise in self-employed telecommuters, this chapter has a range of activities for remote-based teams to use so they can get to know each other and work together just as in-person teams do.

To be noted, all materials for the activities in this chapter will need an electronic device in order for them to be completed properly i.e. — a computer, laptop, smartphone, or tablet. Also, the time limit may vary per activity for you and your team based on your company's communication policies. Most of these activities could be completed in 10 minutes or less, but because virtual teams communicate through technology, you may need to extend the time or keep it on going so your team members have time to respond.

ICEBREAKERS

341. Let's break the ice

Purpose: Getting to know your team

Group size: Any

Level: First

Materials: Electronic device

Time: 10 minutes (or on-going)

Description: Asking basic questions about one another is always a great ice-breaker, especially for virtual teams. Ask your team members to participate in an open discussion forum, group chat or video chat for this activity (pick the one that works best for your team). Make a list of simple questions for each team member to answer.

For example:

- If you were stranded on an island what would be the top three items you would bring?

- If money were no object, where would you go on vacation and why?

- Do you have a family? If so, tell us about them?

- What are looking forward to most about working for this team and company?

Make the questions as open- or closed-ended as you'd like. Just be sure they are unique but informative at the same time.

342. Reply all

Purpose: Getting to know your team

Group size: Any

Level: First

Materials: Electronic device

Time: On-going

Description: This is a simple icebreaker activity for teams that don't necessarily require video chat to communicate. As the team leader, send out an email with a couple basic introductory questions:

- What's your name and position on the team?

- Where are you from?

- What is one interesting fact about you?

- Where did you go to school?

You can make the questions as simple or challenging as you wish. Ask your team members to hit "reply all" when they answer so everyone can read each other's responses.

343. Three truths and a lie (virtual version)

Purpose: Getting to know your team

Group size: Any

Level: First

Materials: Electronic device

Time: On-going

Description: This game is exactly like the first version in this book except it's played on electronic devices. It can be played via email or video chat. Ask your team members to write down three facts about themselves — two are true and one will be false. They are to take turns sharing their facts and, in turns, they each should try to guess which fact is a lie out of each other's lists.

344. Where are you from?

Purpose: Getting to know your team

Group size: Any

Level: First

Materials: Electronic device

Time: 10 minutes (or on-going)

Description: This game can be played through email, on video chat or a conference call. Ask each player to take turns giving three hints about where they live. It can be the exact city if everyone is aware of it or it can be by state if team members live in various locations around the world. If this game is played through email, ask team members to include three pictures of their city in the body of their email. They are to take turns guessing where each other lives until someone gets it right. To keep time moving, feel free to set a time cap, however. For example, each person gets two guesses and if no one gets it right then the person who is sharing can tell everyone where he or she is from at the end of the round. This is a more vocal icebreaker that is fun to play as an introductory activity for new teams.

345. Two pictures

Purpose: Getting to know your team

Group size: Any

Level: First

Materials: Electronic device and personal photos

Time: 30 minutes

Description: This game works best during a video chat. Ask each team member to share two pictures of him or herself during a video-call meeting. The pictures should not be work related but two images that capture that person's life outside of work. They can be pictures of their families, hobbies, or other activities they enjoy doing. Give each person five minutes to explain his or her photos, along with a little bit of background information about themselves. Encourage others to ask questions about their teammates' background after seeing their photos. Make the activity run longer if you decide to do so.

346. Take a picture of your shoes

Purpose: Getting to know your team

Group size: Any

Level: First/Basic

Materials: Electronic device and shoes

Time: 15 minutes (or on-going)

Description: This activity is also very simple but gives insight to someone's personality. Send an email out to all of your employees and ask them to respond with a picture of what shoes they are wearing at that exact moment (make sure they hit reply all so everyone gets their response). This activity is fun because everyone is most likely wearing different shoes or, maybe, they aren't wearing any. It's quick, to the point, and can start small conversations.

347. Find the common thread

Purpose: Team bonding; getting to know your team

Group size: 12 or less

Level: First/Basic

Materials: Electronic devices

Time: 15 minutes (or on-going)

Description: Depending on how fast you expect responses is how this activity will go. If you decide that your team will work on this activity over a video call, then it will only take about 15 minutes. But if you decide to give your team a deadline to complete this activity, then they can communicate via email, phone, or video to get it done.

Divide your team into smaller groups and tell them they are to find three to five things that they all have in common with each other. It can be a favorite movie, same name, or the fact that they all like dogs. Once they've found their most prominent common thread, they are to make a list if stereotypical qualities that are associated with it. For example, if a group discovered they all to like go shopping, then some qualities they could list are rich, snooty, and attitude.

After each group has completed the activity, discuss via video or conference call how eliminating stereotypes is important in the workplace especially when working on a team.

348. Create a team logo or character

Purpose: Creative thinking

Group size: Any

Level: First/Basic

Materials: Electronic devices and graphic design programs

Time: 20 minutes (or on-going)

Description: Split your team into smaller groups once more and give them a short period of time to come up with a team logo or mascot. For graphic design teams, this activity works well because you can have your small groups create their design on a graphics program like Adobe Creative Suite or even on Word. Other teams who are not so experienced in graphic design can still try to create their logo or mascot on one of these programs or, if they wish, they can draw it on paper and send a picture to their team leader or boss.

This activity is meant to bring your teammates closer together and put their creative thinking skills to the test. Their logo and/or mascot should symbolize what they all think the team represents. Make sure to share the designs with the rest of the team. Ask everyone to vote on the best creation and make it the team's permanent logo or mascot.

349. Gifts and hooks

Purpose: Open communication; getting to know your team

Group size: Any

Level: Any

Materials: Electronic devices

Time: 30 minutes

Description: This activity is great for virtual teams because it encourages open communication right off the bat. It can even be used for teams that have been together for quite some time. The team leader should ask each team member to list three to five "gifts" that they bring to the team i.e. — skills, knowledge, etc.

They should also list three to five "hooks" that they need from the team i.e. — things they need to stay fully engaged. Have each person email the team leader their answers and then openly discuss them at the next meeting where everyone is present (a conference call or video group chat). This way, everyone understands what he or she needs from one another in order to be a well-functioning, healthy team from the start instead of later when work starts to pile high.

350. Care packages

Purpose: Team appreciation

Group size: Any

Level: Any

Materials: Random items that the team leader feels will make a great care package

Time: None

Description: This is not so much an activity as a nice, appreciative gesture done by the team leader or boss. It's always important for upper management to stay connected with its employees and notice their hard work. For virtual teams, it may be a little more challenging because you don't see everyone every day, but it's not impossible. As a team leader or a boss, try sending a care package or thank-you box to your employees when you notice they have been going above and beyond at work. You can also send a care package to a new team member to make them feel more welcomed. The packages do not have to be anything too fancy; gift cards, food, office supplies, and a handwritten note would suffice.

IGNITE THE FLAME

351. Rotational leadership

Purpose: Team support and leadership skills

Group size: Eight to 15

Level: Any

Materials: None

Time: None

Description: It's always important to give people a chance at leading a team especially at work. For different projects, either choose or let team members volunteer to be the team leader for specific project. There can be multiple team leaders on one project if it calls for multiple responsibilities such as communications, budgeting, or planning. Make sure everyone has had a turn to be a team leader before starting the process all over again. This exercise is ongoing and helps employees break out of their comfort zones.

352. Shared learning

Purpose: Team support and engagement

Group size: Any

Level: Any

Materials: Electronic devices

Time: To be determined by activity

Description: There are always multiple events that employees and team members alike can attend to advance their knowledge about a certain topic. These events can be webinars or conferences. However, smaller things such as business articles or research papers also advance people's knowledge just as well.

Find a webinar, convention, or article that two or more team members can read or attend together. After they have completed their assigned task, ask them to share what they learned with the rest of the team. Ask them to listen or look for tips that they think the team would benefit from as a whole. Connect via, phone, conference call, or video chat so everyone can listen in on the shared knowledge for that week.

353. Fear in a hat

Purpose: Building team support

Group size: Any

Level: First/Basic

Materials: Electronic devices

Time: 20 minutes

Description: Similar to the in-person version, team members will write down any fears they have about being on the team or for upcoming projects. The only difference is these fears will be emailed to the team leader or boss instead of written anonymously on a piece of paper. During the next team meeting, the team leader will address each fear anonymously and further support and comfort the entire team about each one. This will help ease the team's mind altogether without throwing anyone under the bus.

354. What could go wrong?

Purpose: Creative thinking

Group size: 10 or less

Level: Any

Materials: Electronic devices

Time: 15 minutes

Description: To spark some creativity within your team members, ask them to come up with their own story at the next group meeting. The team leader should start the story off with one or two sentences and then the next person should follow suit. The process keeps repeating until the team leader calls time. This activity can get entertaining really fast because it's up to each team member to contribute something new to the story. At the end of the activity, have a discussion about the importance of creativity, taking risks, and innovation. Talk about why all of those aspects are important for your team members to consider as they take on new projects and assignments within the company.

355. Celebrate 5th Fridays

Description: There are a few months out of the year that have five Friday's instead of four. When they occur, celebrate the day with your work family. Play games or treat everyone to lunch by sending them a gift card. By doing so, team leaders are letting their employees know that they are appreciated. Incorporate a few team building activities on these days also to make the day signify teamwork and team bonding.

GAMES

356. Whose office is it anyway?

Purpose: Getting to know your teammates

Group size: Any

Level: First

Materials: Electronic devices and a file sharing tool

Time: On-going

Description: This activity is very simple but a lot of fun. Ask each team member to take a picture of his or her home office and upload it to a shareable file. Tell them that they should leave their desks and working space as is to give a feel for how they are. For example, coffee mugs, open blinds and papers everywhere should be left untouched before the photo is taken. It makes the activity more mysterious this way. Someone's office could be a table at a local coffee shop or their sofa. Give everyone a deadline to complete the assignment so during the next virtual meeting everyone can try to guess which office picture belongs to whom.

357. Conference call trivia

Purpose: Getting to know your team

Group size: 4 to 8 people per group

Level: Any

Materials: Trivia questions and an electronic device

Time: 30 minutes

Description: Divide your team into smaller groups and send them each a sheet of trivia questions. For 30 minutes, ask them to play conference-call trivia and learn about each other's personalities and interests outside of work. This activity can be useful for newly formed teams or for teams who know each but have only worked together for a short period of time. It gives them a break from work-related assignments to relax with their teammates.

358. Online Catchphrase or Charades

Purpose: Team bonding

Group size: 10 or less

Level: First/Basic

Materials: Virtual charades cards or a similar resource

Time: 30 minutes

Description: Split your team in half for two teams. They will be competing against each other in a virtual game of charades or catchphrase. The team leader can monitor the game via video call, which is how everyone will be communicating and playing the game. The game does not have to be too long but just enough time for everyone to get a turn and for the team leader to count the score. This activity can be a fun way to end a long week or introduce new team members to one another.

359. Virtual bingo

Purpose: Team bonding

Group size: 10 or less

Level: Any

Materials: Bingo cards (emailed to each player), questions and an electronic device with video and a microphone

Time: 15 to 20 minutes

Description: The team leader should create a bingo card ad email it to everyone to either print out or keep track of his or her answers online. The team leader should come up with a list of questions that are related to work, the company, or recent projects. Play this game on a Friday afternoon to end the week on a fun note and make sure everyone can play via Skype, FaceTime, or another video-chat program that every team member has access to. Offer prizes for the winners, which will be mailed to them after the game has ended.

360. Virtual diversity bingo

Purpose: Team bonding, open communication, and acceptance

Group size: 10 or less

Level: Any

Materials: Bingo cards (emailed to each player), questions, and an electronic device with video and a microphone

Time: 15 to 20 minutes

Description: This game will function exactly the same as the one above, so for further tips and directions read above. However, the purpose behind the game is different. After you have conducted a few rounds of diversity bingo, lead a conversation about why diversity is important and how it helps the team's success.

The questions for this game should be related to different cultures, religions and ways of life.

For example, a few questions could be:

- Do you celebrate a holiday in December that is not Christmas?

- Do you pray more than twice a day?

- Did you have the opportunity to go to school full-time when you were younger or did you have to work as well?

Make sure your questions are serious questions and are not meant to mock or make fun of anyone's culture or way of life. This game is about accepting those who may be different than us and why it's important to have that understanding as a team.

361. Virtual scavenger hunt

Purpose: Getting to know your company programs

Group size: Any

Level: First

Materials: Computer or laptop and accessible files, programs, folders, and documents

Time: 20 minutes

Description: This activity can be altered depending on the reasons for doing the activity, but it's a great introductory game for new team members, especially virtual teams. If your company uses multiple programs, shared files and folders, and documents, then this game can be useful for new employees.

Create a scavenger hunt asking team members to locate certain files, toolbars, documents, spreadsheets, etc. that employees use at the company on a daily basis. This way, the new team members can familiarize themselves with the company's policies and expectations, as well as the software required for them to use. Send a cheat sheet or an answer key should they get stuck or cannot find the item they are supposed to find.

362. Virtual speed dating

Purpose: Icebreaker

Group size: 12 or less

Level: First

Materials: A timer and an electronic device with a microphone or video camera

Time: 30 minutes (depending on the size of the team)

Description: Similar to in-person speed dating, virtual speed dating gives team members a certain amount of time to get to know their coworkers. This can be tricky as a virtual team, but an idea is to have everyone play on a conference call or on a video sharing application that allows people to mute others on the call. This activity is always a great way to introduce new people to one another or introduce old team members to new ones. Make sure all of the technical glitches have been figured out before the game — you wouldn't want one bad thing to prevent the entire activity from happening.

VIRTUAL MEET-UPS

363. Virtual coffee break or happy hour

Purpose: Team bonding

Group size: Any

Level: Any

Materials: Electronic device and a beverage

Time: 15 to 30 minutes

Description: This activity will work really with teams that have members spread out all over the country or the world. Find a common time that everyone can take 15 to 30 minutes out of his or her week to sit down and participate in a virtual coffee break or happy hour. It can be challenging if multiple people live in different time zones, but the leader should try to persuade as many people to participate as possible. This allows teams to talk about other things besides work on a weekly basis and it promotes a strong sense of team recognition, relaxation, and bonding.

364. Virtual team lunch or dinner

Purpose: Team bonding

Group size: Any

Level: Any

Materials: Electronic device and food

Time: 30 to 45 minutes

Description: If you're looking for an activity to spend more time together, try planning a time where everyone can have a virtual meal together. As mentioned earlier in this book, eating, without a doubt, brings people together. Ask your team members to make the same dish at their homes for this activity. It will be fun to compare dishes and see what people paired with it or how they cooked it.

365. Catch up via video call

Purpose: Team bonding

Group size: 10 or less

Level: Any

Materials: Electronic device with a camera and microphone

Time: 10 minutes

Description: Every Monday, start the week off with a video conference call. For the first 10 minutes, catch up with the rest of the team. Ask members what they did over the weekend, how their projects are coming along, or if they have any fun news to share. Encourage others to ask questions as well; the team leader should not be the only one asking questions. This promotes a sense of team bonding and relaxation before jumping into work for the week.

Conclusion

Team building activities can seem like a waste of time at first if not initiated with the right attitude from upper management. It's important for team leaders, bosses, presidents, and directors to participate and lead in all team building activities — especially with new teams or with teams experiencing major conflicts.

The activities in this book can bring teammates closer together, creating stronger bonds that make it easier for them to trust one another, collaborate, work together, and even fail together. All of these successes can be achieved if just one team leader takes the first step. A team's end outcomes are only as successful as the people who put in the work on that team.

INDIVIDUAL BENEFITS

Stronger teams are not the only result of team building activities; individual's can feel more confident in themselves and in their work after they participate in a team building exercise, because they challenge themselves to step out of their comfort zones. Stepping out of one's comfort zone leads to self-discovery and stronger self-esteem — two qualities any team leader should want their employees to experience.

> Team building activities that challenge participants to get outside their comfort zone are great at building self-esteem. These challenges tend to be physically demanding, like walking on a log 30 feet in the air while attached to a belay, or moving each member of the group through a "spider's web." The transformation of the individual from being timid about the activity to the huge smile and excitement of accomplishing the task is awesome.
> — *Deb Dowling*

Creating new challenges helps team members learn to work together to complete them, which results in tighter bonds of trust. Team members' self-esteem and self-discovery are important for a well-functioning team. If individuals feel good about what they are accomplishing — both individually and as part of a larger team — then they will be more motivated to not only continue their hard work and dedication but also strive to accomplish even more.

CHECKING IN

It is up to the leader to monitor how team members are doing, which can be done in a variety of ways.

Depending on the work circumstance and the type of team, checking in can be a very powerful technique. A check-in by the leader of the group can be daily, weekly, or monthly. The more frequent the check, the more reliable the team leader seems.

During the check-in, the leader should start off with a positive remark like:

> "You really went above and beyond the call of duty yesterday" *or* "I was really impressed with how you dealt with your team member during the crisis today."

This sets the stage as a positive one rather than a negative one. This can be followed with whatever topic needs to be addressed. Your statement should still start off with a positive.

Do not start a conversation off like the example below:

> "I have noticed you are not pulling your load. You are really adding to your team members' workload."

A better statement is:

> "I noticed you have been working hard at your job. Have you considered trying to speed up your production? It would really help out the team, and they can help you with some of your other duties."

This way the individual is included as part of the team, rather than being singled out as an individual. They can identify as a team member. It is important, however, that team members understand that they are responsible for their daily tasks, which is why checking in should be implemented in a team leader's weekly agenda. By checking in, you can make your employees feel like an important member of the team as opposed to someone who just has a personal responsibility. It is easier to make excuses for our own individual mistakes than to let down others on a team.

MOTIVATION

Believe it or not, team building activities can lead to more motivated employees or team members. Being part of a successful team can be a powerful feeling.

In 1943, a well-known psychologist, Abraham Maslow, published a groundbreaking study called A Theory of Human Motivation. In the paper, Maslow suggested what has become known as the hierarchy of needs. This pyramid contains a set of human needs that motivates human beings and accounts for many human behaviors.

Below is the list of needs that Maslow discovered, ranging from basic to higher psychological needs. Maslow suggests that every human has this same pyramid of needs and that we can jump from one level to another at different times.

Maslow suggests that, if the first four needs are not met, we feel anxious. The reason this is included in this book is that members of your team are affected daily by every one of these needs. If you can recognize symptoms of deficiency, you can help your team members get back on track. If these needs are not met, humans become distracted and focus on their needs until they are met.

Utilize the exercises in this book to your benefit and don't be afraid to try a new one with your team. The more time your team spends together, the stronger their bond will become. Encourage creativity and laughing, along with comfort and support, because the more familiar your members are with one another the more successful they will be in both individual and team pursuits. Virtual teams have this opportunity, too. Do not assume that technology prevents teams from being strong and successful; they are capable of achieving the same greatness as in-person teams.

> There are always moments in these types of exercises where everyone starts laughing uncontrollably. Go with it. Don't try to get control of the group. Let them laugh, as laughing together is one of the best team building exercises ever. — *Kim Stinson*

CONTACTS

Kim Stinson

Kim Stinson holds an M.F.A. in Playwriting from Spalding University, an M.A. in Theatre from Miami University (Oxford, Ohio), and a B.F.A. in technical theatre from the North Carolina School of the Arts. Having been a professional stage manager, directed a few plays, and taught a few theatre courses, she is currently writing plays for fun, but not much profit.

The majority of Kim's team building experience is through theatre-related activities. Theatre is a natural place for exploration and experimentation with team building exercises. Everyone is gathered for a few weeks to a few months for the same goal: that of putting a piece of entertainment on the stage for the benefit of an audience. Actors use team building exercises all the time in classes and in rehearsals. Improvisations are natural team building exercises, as are singing or vocal exercises and movement-oriented exercises. In a non-theatrical setting, no one need be a singer or a dancer, but merely to allow themselves to say things out loud and to move around themselves and each other. Just getting up and doing something together helps team members form connections and bonds, as well as understand each other better.

Pramod Goel

Pramod Goel has extensive experience building business practices in startup, growth, and turnaround phases of the company across multiple industries, such as healthcare, airlines, nuclear, oil and gas, and manufacturing. While serving in senior management capacities with leading firms, he has delivered many strategic and tactical enterprise solutions encompassing operational restructuring, business process reengineering, and enterprise application implementation.

Goel's management consulting experience includes operational assessment, enterprise business modeling, change management, program management, business analytics, mathematical/operations research modeling, departmental infrastructure building, group facilitation/JAD, channel management, and implementation methodologies, while creating superior customer relationships.

Goel has strong cross-industry experience, delivering business solutions to Fortune 500 clients including Air Products & Chemicals, Alyeska, American Airlines, Anheuser-Busch, Australian Government, British Airways, British Energy, Continental Airlines, Ford, Flextronics, Huntsman, Jabil/Varian, Kerr McGee, Occidental Chemicals, Omaha Public Power, PECO Energy, Phoenix International/John Deere, Procter & Gamble, Qwest, State Farm, and Veterans Health Administration.

Goel holds a master's degree in Industrial & Systems Engineering and a bachelor's degree in Mechanical Engineering. Mr. Goel has built both internal (within the company) and external (at customer site) teams for over 16 years under different business environments.

Stephen G. F. Coenen

Stephen is the Human Resources Generalist at Covidien, Inc. (formerly Tyco Healthcare) in St. Louis, Missouri. He has worked at Coiden for three years. Before that, he was a member of the Human Resources staff at Saft America, Inc. for almost four years.

Stephen holds an M.A. Industrial Organizational Psychology and Human Resources Management from Appalachian State University. He received his B.S. in Psychology at Western Carolina University.

Stephen has been involved in training and team building activities for years as part of his human resource positions. He has been involved in various volunteer community organizations and is currently the President of the Greenleaf Singers, a renaissance singing group based in St. Louis.

Breon M. Klopp

Breon is the Senior Director of Development at PIT Instruction & Training. Breon is the founder and Senior Director of a motor sports facility in Mooresville, North Carolina (Race City, USA), providing pit crew team building and lean performance training programs for groups and corporations. He is a former instructor and coach for professional motor sports pit crews in NASCAR®.

The programs provided by PIT are based on the concept that, if individuals and organizations were managed and operated using the same principles that guide highly competitive racing pit crews, organizations would be more efficient, effective, and profitable.

PIT has provided award-winning (2006 Elliott Masie Learning Consortium Innovative Leadership Award /2007 North Carolina Small Business of the Year Finalist) motor sports related team building programs since 2001 and has served a large number of local, national, and international organizations, including United Airlines, Intel, ConocoPhillips, Union Pacific, PalletOne, Blue Ridge Paper Corporation, Georgia Pacific, and Textron.

PIT also provides services to teaching organizations, including the North Carolina Youth Advisory Council, the Ford/AAA Student Auto Skills competition, Jostens Yearbook conferences, and school career days, including Grier Middle School, recipient of the Time Warner National Award for a physics and math teaching unit based on NASCAR®. PIT is primarily a professional pit crew training facility for competitive teams in NASCAR®.

Deb Dowling

Deb is the Vice President of Program Services/Property/Camp Director of Girl Scout Council of the Catawba Valley Area. Deb directs Camp Ginger Cascades, Lenoir, North Carolina, which is owned and operated since 1963 by the Girl Scout Council of the Catawba Valley Area, 530 4th Street SW, Hickory, North Carolina. The web site is **www.cvgirlscouts.org.** The 265-acre camp is located in the Brushy Mountains. It includes sleeping and program facilities of winterized cabins, lodges, and tree houses. The camp has a dining hall with an institutional kitchen, a small lake for canoeing and kayaking, a swimming pool, a natural water slide on Ginger Creek, a challenge course, and a climbing wall. Deb has used team building activities at events, conferences, meetings, camps, and trainings with Girl Scouts, summer camp staff, Girl Scout events serving 15 to 1,200 participants, volunteers in Girl Scouting, troop leaders, and parents and girl/adult committees working on specific projects. She has used initiative games, low/high challenge courses, and climbing towers. Team building activities are a part of most events in Girl Scouting

Michelle Lovejoy

Michelle Lovejoy received a B.A. in Geology, Mathematics, and Anthropology from Appalachian State University in 1999. During her undergraduate program, she participated in a research project involving glacial marine sedimentation from the Vancouver Island area. She worked as a Project Geologist for a consulting firm in Ohio, focusing on Phase I & II Environmental Site Assessments, wetland delineation and mitigation projects, groundwater remediation, NEPA, and cultural resource inventory reviews for cellular tower sites. She obtained an MS in Environmental and Engineering Geosciences from Radford University in 2004. She is currently employed by the North Carolina Department of Environment and Natural Resources, Division of Soil and Water Conservation as a Senior Environmental Scientist. She works directly with 13 local soil and water conservation districts to assist with the implementation of cost-share programs and educational outreach. She also assists with the delivery of statewide training and conferences, grant writing, and implementing Soil and Water Conservation Commission policies. She also manages the statewide contract local soil and water conservation districts have with the Ecosystem Enhancement Program, North Carolina's wetland mitigation program for the Department of Transportation. She is a prospective 2007 fellow of the Natural Resources Leadership Institute, with a project focusing on developing a training manual and delivering a round of workshops providing tools for local districts to be actively involved in farmland preservation including conservation easement programs.

As a teenager, she participated in many summer programs and leadership training activities that utilized team building activities to introduce everyone and develop friendships at the start of the event. As a senior environmental scientist, she is responsible for development of agendas for statewide, regional, and local meetings and trainings. She uses many of the team building exercises mentioned in this book and often starts meetings off with a quick exercise to get everyone focused.

Glossary

Collaboration: The action of working with someone to produce or create something.

Productivity: The effectiveness of productive effort, especially in industry, as measured in terms of the rate of output per unit of input.

Conflicts: Serious disagreement or argument, typically a protracted one.

Deficiency: A failing or shortcoming; or a lack or shortage.

Diversity: Variety; a range of different things.

Ethics: Moral principles that govern a person's or group's behavior.

Icebreaker: A game, exercise, or activity that serves to relieve inhibitions or tension between people or start a conversation.

Innovative: Featuring new methods; advanced and original; or (of a person) introducing new ideas; original and creative in thinking.

Maslow's Hierarchy of Needs: A description of the needs that motivate human behavior. In 1943, Abraham Maslow proposed five different kinds of human needs, beginning with the most basic: survival. Physiological needs, such as food and shelter, are followed by needs related to safety.

Morale: The confidence, enthusiasm, and discipline of a person or group at a particular time.

Motivation: The general desire or willingness of someone to do something.

Project teams: Temporary teams created to complete a specific project.

Remote teams: A group of individuals who work across time, space, and organizational boundaries with links strengthened by webs of communication technology.

Root cause analysis: A systematic process for identifying "root causes" of problems or events and an approach for responding to them. It is based on the basic idea that effective management requires more than merely "putting out fires" for problems that develop, but finding a way to prevent them.

Self-actualization: The realization or fulfillment of one's talents and potentialities especially considered as a drive or need present in everyone.

Stereotype: A widely held but fixed and oversimplified image or idea of a particular type of person or thing.

Team building: A collective term for various types of activities used to enhance social relations and define roles within teams, often involving collaborative tasks. It is distinct from team training, which is designed to improve the efficiency, rather than interpersonal relations.

Telecommute: Work from home, making use of the internet, email, and the telephone.

Time-management: The ability to use one's time effectively or productively, especially at work.

Upper management: Individuals and teams that are responsible for making the primary decisions within a company.

Values: The regard that something is held to deserve; the importance, worth, or usefulness of something.

Virtual teams: Teams that work together by using technology to communicate, collaborate, and bond.

Working teams: More permanent teams that work together every day.

Bibliography

"10 Quick and Easy Team Building Activities [Part 1]." *Huddle*. Web. 12 Sept.   2016.

"10 Team-Building Games That Promote Collaborative Critical Thinking." *TeachThought*. 23 June 2016. Web. 12 Sept. 2016.

Analytics, Global Workplace. "Federal Telework – Return on Taxpayer Investment."   *Global Workplace Analytics*. Web. 12 Sept. 2016.

Billig, Aubrielle. "24 Team Building Games and Exercises." *Small Business Trends*. 22 Sept. 2015. Web. 12 Sept. 2016.

Bonnie, Emily. "Ultimate Guide to Team Building Activities That Don't Suck." *Blog Wrike*. 08 Sept. 2016. Web. 12 Sept. 2016.

"Building a Collaborative Team Environment." *U.S. Office of Personnel Management*. Web. 12 Sept. 2016.

"Communication and Listening Exercises." *Trainers Warehouse Blog Comments*. 09 Sept. 2016. Web. 12 Sept. 2016.

"Global Vote Exercise." *High Performance Teams*. Web. 12 Sept. 2016.

Gordon, Jon. "My Favorite Team Building Exercises." *My Favorite Team Building Exercises*. Web. 12 Sept. 2016.

Higgins, Chris. "5 Icebreakers for Distributed Team Meetings." *5 Icebreakers for Distributed Team Meetings.* Web. 12 Sept. 2016.

McDuffee, Samantha. "Out of Sight, Out of Mind? 5 Virtual Team Bonding Tips for Remote Employees." *TeamBonding.* 27 July 2016. Web. 12 Sept. 2016.

"Office Games for Employees." *Buzzle.* Buzzle.com. Web. 12 Sept. 2016.

Osborne, Mary. "Positive Thinking Games." LIVESTRONG.COM. LIVESTRONG.COM 19, Apr. 2015. Web.

"Pet Statistics." *ASPCA.* Web. 15 Sept. 2016.

Services, Management Consulting. ""Who's Got a Dollar?" Exercise." *Who's Got a Dollar? Exercise.* Web. 12 Sept. 2016.

Soon, Wendy. "13 Top Team Building Activities." *Virtual Workspace.* 2014. Web.

"Take a Deep Breath." *The American Institute of Stress.* Web. 15 Sept. 2016.

"The 6 Best Company Team Building Activities to Build Workplace Camaraderie." *Insider Monkey Free Hedge Fund and Insider Trading Data RSS.* Web. 12 Sept. 2016.

"Team Building Activities." *Challenges Venture Team Building.* Web. 12 Sept. 2016.

"The Food Project: Youth. Food. Community." *Communication Activities.* Web. 12 Sept. 2016.

"The Team Building Directory." *Free Team Building Activities Comments.* Web. 12 Sept. 2016.

Work, By Life Meets. "10 Team Building Exercises for Remote/Virtual/Dispersed Teams - Life Meets Work." *Life Meets Work.* 25 July 2016. Web. 12 Sept. 2016.

Wormley, Rob. "An Epic List of Great Team Building Games." *When I Work.* 16 Feb. 2016. Web. 12 Sept. 2016.

Zaina Ghabra on August 23, 2012 in Leadership and Management, Teamwork and Communication. "Six Quick Teamwork Games to Engage Employees at Work." Web. 12 Sept. 2016.

Index